FIRST THOUGHT
BEST THOUGHT

Photo by George Holmes

CHÖGYAM TRUNGPA

First Thought
Best Thought

108 Poems

Edited by David I. Rome

Introduction by Allen Ginsberg

SHAMBHALA
Boulder & London 1983

SHAMBHALA PUBLICATIONS INC.
1920 13th Street
Boulder, Colorado 80302

© 1983 by Chögyam Trungpa

9 8 7 6 5 4 3 2 1
First Edition
All rights reserved.

Distributed in the United States by Random House
and in Canada by Random House of Canada Ltd.
Distributed in the United Kingdom by Routledge & Kegan Paul Ltd.,
London and Henley-on-Thames.

Printed in the United States of America.

LIBRARY OF CONGRESS CATALOGING IN PUBLICATION DATA
Trungpa, Chögyam, 1939–
    First thought, best thought.

    1. Buddhist poetry, American.   I. Title.
PS3570.R84F5   1983   811'.54   83-42806
ISBN 0-87773-092-X (*pbk.*)
ISBN 0-394-73269-3 (Random House; *pbk.*)

This book is dedicated to Milarepa, the poet-yogi of the Kagyü lineage, who has inspired me since my childhood.

CONTENTS

INTRODUCTION

AS LINEAGE HOLDER in Ear-whispered Kagyü transmission of Tibetan Buddhist practice of Wakefulness, Chögyam Trungpa is "Rinpoche" or "Precious Jewel" of millenial practical information on attitudes and practices of mind speech & body that Western Poets over the same millenia have explored, individually, fitfully, as far as they were able—searching thru cities, scenes, seasons, manuscripts, libraries, backalleys, whorehouses, churches, drawing rooms, revolutionary cells, opium dens, merchant's rooms in Harrar, salons in Lissadell.

Rimbaud, drawing on the Magician Eliphas Levi & hashishien backalleys of Paris, rediscovered "Alchemy of the Verb" and other Western magics including home-made Colors of Vowels & "long reasoned derangement of all the senses" as part of his scheme to arrive at the Unknown as Poet-seer. His conception of Poet as Visionary Savant is unbeatable ambition no Western poet can bypass, tho as in the lives of Rimbaud & Kerouac, mature suffering, the First Noble Truth of existence, may be the destined end of ambitious magic. Some Reality is arrived at: "Charity is that key—This inspiration proves that I have dreamed! . . . I who called myself angel or seer, exempt from all morality, I am returned to the soil with a duty to seek and rough reality to embrace! Peasant!"

Rimbaud, still a model of the Beautiful Poet, concluded his life's last year with the following letters: "In the long run our life is a horror, an endless horror! What are we alive for?" . . . "My life is over, all I am now is a motionless stump." Generations later poets are still trying to change Reality with the Revolution of the Word, a XX Century preoccupation drawing on Western gnostic sources.

Some compromise with Absolute Truth had to be made in XX Century poetics: W.C. Williams thru Kerouac, poets were willing to work with relative truth, the sight at hand, accurate perception of appearance, accurate reportage of consciousness—although Hart Crane & some Rock Poets continued to force the issue of Self-Immolation as means of becoming One with phenomena.

As part of the aesthetics of working with relative truth, an American idiom developed (born out of the spacious pragmatism of Whit-man in dealing with his own Ego): The acceptance of actual poetic (poesis: making) behavior of the mind as model, subject, & measure of literary form and content. Mind is shapely, Art is shapely. Ger-trude Stein's style thus merges literary artifact with present conscious-ness during the time of composition. Put another way: the sequence of events of poet's mind, accidents of mind, provide the highlights, jumps & Plot of Poetry. As to the Muse, "She's there, installed amid the kitchenware" as Whitman celebrated the change from Absolute Heroic to Relative Honesty in poetic method. Thus we inherited our world of poetry in XX Century.

Thirst for some Absolute Truth still lurks behind this shift, thus Bullfighting, Drugs, God, Communism, Realpolitik or Revolution, Drink, Suburb or Bohemia, Sex, grassroots communalism, ecology or Amerindian ground, blasts of Eternal Vision, Death's Skull, even various Apocalypses or Extraterrestrial Paranoias & delights recur as our preoccupation, and have been epic'd. Brave energies of fear, joy or anomia, not much certainty; yet there's been honest effort to display what can be seen of naked mind, and that's led to an amaz-ingly open style of Poetry which includes snow-blinding Sierras and rain-diamonded traffic lights, as mind's-eye does. An international style, based on facts, has emerged, perhaps the most relaxed poetic mode ever. Still, no certainty emerges but ultimate suffering, acceler-ating change, and perhaps some vast glimpse of universal soullessness. Has the poetic Seer failed? Or perhaps succeeded at arriving at a place of beat bleakness where the ego of Poetry is annihilated?

At last! To the Rescue! Carrying the panoply of 25 centuries of wakened mind-consciousness "where glorious radiant Howdahs/are being carried by elephants/through groves of flowing milk/past para-dises of Waterfall/into the valley of bright gems/be rubying an antique ocean/floor of undiscovered splendor/in the heart of un happiness."* And Whozat? The poet of absolute Sanity and resolution, "having drunk the hot blood of the ego." The author is a reincarnated Tibetan Lama trained from age 2 in various ancient practices aimed at concentrating attention, focusing perception, minding thought-forms to transparency, profounding awareness, vasting consciousness,

*That's Kerouac's Wish-fulfilling gem, *Mexico City Blues,* 110th Chorus, (New York: Grove Press, 1959).

annihilating ego, & immolating ego-mind in phenomena: a wizard in control of day-dream, conscious visualization & thought projection, vocal sound vibration, outward application of insight, practice of natural virtues, and a very admiral of oceanic scholarship thereof.

The dramatic situation of someone who has realized the World as pure mind, & gone beyond attachment to ego to return to the world & work with universal ignorance, confront the spiritual-materialist daydream of Western world—and tell it in modernist poetry—provides the historic excitement this book puts in our laps.

To focus on one aspect of the drama, consider the progression of style, from early poems adapted out of Tibetan formal-classic modes, to the free-wheeling Personism improvisations of the poems of 1975, which reflect Guru mind's wily means of adapting techniques of Imagism, post-surrealist humor, modernist slang, subjective frankness & egoism, hip "fingerpainting," & tenderhearted spontaneities as adornments of tantric statement. We see respect & appreciation given to the "projective field" of modern Western poetry; this is a teaching in itself, which few past "Gurus" have been able to manifest in their mistier mystic musings. Something has jerked forward here, into focus, visible, in our own language: rare perceptions dealt with in our own terms.

By hindsight the classical style poems become precious exhibitions of cultural starting place & intention for the poet, Chögyam, "the stray dog."

For those familiar with advanced Buddhist practice & doctrine, the solidified symbolisms of early poems are significant teachings, or statements of method, attitude, & experience, as in "The Zen Teacher," where horse, boat and stick may represent Hinayana Mahayana & Vajrayana attitudes of wakefulness. Quite thrilling, unusual, to find a contemporary poet who's master of an ancient "system." Within my memory, it was Academically fashionable to say that the XX Century lacked the culture for great Poetry, not possessing, as Dante's time did, a "system" of cultural assumptions on which to hang an epic. But it seemed too late to go back and clothe the skeleton of God, tho Eliot, Claudel & others yearned nostalgic for such divine certainty.

Chögyam Trungpa, however, does have a Classical system working for him to make "the snakeknot of conceptual mind uncoil in air."

Vajrayana Buddhist symbolism is at his disposal, including the notion of "Absolute Truth"—a property hitherto unclaimable since
Plato kicked the poets out of his republic. Tho' Keats did propose
redeeming Truth as Beauty. Blake created a symbolic sacred world
in many ways parallel to Vajrayana. How do other poet friends look
in this light, faced with contest from within their ranks by poet who's
also lineage holder of the most esoteric teachings of the East? Will
Auden seem amateur, pursuing testy quasi-christian personal conclusions? Does Eliot quote Buddha, Krishna & Christ like a country
vicar? How do I sit, charlatan pedant full of resentful Ginsberghood,
posed by contemporary media as cultural Guru? Does Yeats gasp like
a beached fish in the thin air of Theosophy's "Secret Doctrines" version of the Great East? Whereas "Chögyam writing a poem is like a
king inspecting his Soldiers." Well, Well!

What will poetry readers think of that bardic boast? Diamond
Macho the *Kalevala* song men wouldn't match, tho' they might
threaten to sing each other into a swamp.* What image of Poet!
What would angelic Shelly've said? What would Blake warn? "I
must make a system of my own, or be enslaved by another man's"?
On Mt. Ida the Muses look up astonished by this bolt of lightning
thru blue cloudless sky.

This book is evidence of a Buddha-natured child taking first verbal
steps age 35, in totally other language direction than he spoke age 10,
talking side of mouth slang: redneck, hippie, chamber of commerce,
good citizen, Oxfordian aesthete slang, like a dream Bodhisattva
with thousand eyes & mouths talking turkey.

Thus poems of June 1972 approach the theme of personal love
using open Western forms and "first thought best thought" improvi-
satory technique—statements which mediate between the formality
of Dharma Master and a man immersed in Relative Truth. Phrases
return and re-echo in mind: "Take a thistle to bed,/And make love
to it." The following "Letter to Marpa," classical theme, is done
in smooth mixture of old and new styles: "Ordering Damema to
serve beer for a break." If you know the wife of Marpa (translator
and early founder of Kagyü Lineage) & Trungpa Rinpoche, this

The Kalevala, tr. F.P. MaGoun Jr. (Cambridge, Mass.: Harvard University
Press, 1963), poem 3, 21-330 . . . "up to his teeth behind a rotten tree trunk."

poem's a historic prophecy of transplantation of lineage to America in American terms: awesome knowledge & self-aware humor are explicit in the poem.

"Nameless Child": "hearing the pearl dust crunch between his teeth" is startling statement of egolessness, "unborn nature" of consciousness, done in traditional style. The next experiment is with gnomic haiku-like riddles, developing 7 November 1972 into precise American style "red wheelbarrow" snapshots. "Skiing in a red & blue outfit, drinking cold beer," etc. Thru these we see ordinary mind of the poet, whose specialty as Eastern Teacher is Ordinary Mind.

Years later ordinary egoless mind says in response to anxiety-ridden ecology freaks, "Glory be to the rain/That brought down/Concentrated pollution/On the roof of my car/In the parking lot." Amazing chance to see his thought process step by step, link by link, cutting through solidifications of opinion & fixations on "Badgood-good/goodbadbad" & attachment to this and that humorless image the poems July 1974, including "Ginsberg being Pedantic."

This method of first-thought concatenations develops in a series of tipsy essays in modern style—some dealing with serious personal matters. By September 1974, in "Supplication to the Emperor," Ancient Wisdom Transmission heritage is wedded to powerful modern "surrealist" style.

These poems are dictated amidst an ocean of other activities including the utterance of masses of books of Dharma exposition—as the Tibetan imagery says "a mountain of jewels"—exactly true of this strange poet in our midst, noticing our "Aluminum-rim black leather executive chairs."

What's odd, adventurous, inventive, mind-blowing, is the combination of classical occasion (visit of head of Kagyü Order, His Holiness Gyalwa Karmapa, to North America) treated in authentic post-Apollinaire recognizably American-minded style ("Supplication to the Emperor").

Poignant and powerful then, the re-echoes of liturgical style that reappear in 1974, the poet in midst of struggle with the flypaper of modern centerless-minded poetics: (as in an unpublished text, "Homage to Samantabhadra," 11 November 1974)

I am a mad Yogi.
Since I have no beginning, no end,
I am known as the ocean of Dharma.
I am the primordial madman;
I am primordially drunk.
Since all comes from me,
I am the only son of the only Guru.

By February 1975, a series of poems in entirely modern style indicate absorption of the lively fashion of versifying developed in the U.S. after models of Christopher Smart & Apollinaire, & transmitted in U.S. '50s to '70s by Corso, the "List Poem" spoken of by Anne Waldman and others—see the cadenzas punning and joking on the word Palm (25 February 1975), the "best minds" commentary of the same day, and subsequent love poems. In "Dying Laughing" there's an ironic commentary on modern poetic mind, "scattered thoughts are the best you can do . . . That the whole universe/could be exasperated/And die laughing."

There follows a series of portraits—"characters" as T.S. Eliot termed certain of W.C. Williams' poems on persons—thumbnail sketches of his students, their natures exposed to X-ray humorous advice—"If you're going to tickle me, be gentle. . . But titillating enough to stimulate my system with your feminine healthy shining well-trimmed nail just so . . ."

Of the famous situation of Guru playing with disciples this is rare honest private occasion made public where you can see the inside story & its humanity & innocence, its true teaching & bone quick insight. Tiny details of personality, irritating seen in greater space, along with tiny details of resolution of problems of egoic self-consciousness proposed by subjects of the portraits—this one composed March 1975:

> *. . . jalapeño dumpling*
> *Bitten by Alice's white teeth,*
> *Which are lubricated by feminine saliva*

There's an odd reminder of Kurt Schwitters' *Anne Blume* here, or: the love poem dated 7 March 1975:

As she turns her head
From the little irritation of long flowing hair
She says, Mmmm.
But on the other hand she is somewhat perturbed;
Not knowing whether she is glamorous or ugly

A number of successful complete poems follow, the poetic ground having been prepared, the improvisational practice having been taken seriously, thus "Victory Chatter" is fruition of poetic path begun consciously much earlier. The details in the mind of the "good general" of dharma battle are recognizable. A number of poems like "Missing the Point" have extra flavor of inside gossip on attitudes & thought processes of the professional teacher, "Lingering thought/Tells me/My private secretary is really drunk" & have sort of Chinese Royal tone; might've been written in 14th Century Kham slang. "RMDC": "Dead or alive, I have no regrets." An up-to-date playfulness develops, mind-plays of obvious charm, even naivete, as in writings by Marsden Hartley or Samuel Greenberg's not-well-known classics.

"Report from Loveland," July 1975: The whole dharma is given in Disneyesque parody of everyday perplexity's Bourgeois life. By that month's end, the writings are well-formed shapes with one subject. The "1135 10th St." lady friend poem is a series of exquisitely courteous & penetrant, yet funny, first thoughts, where mind's mixed with dharma and every noticed detail points in a unified direction. Can you, by following first thoughts, arrive at a rounded complete one-subject poem, but crazy-poetic still, like: "fresh air/Which turns into a well-cared-for garden/Free from lawnmowers and insecticides?"

In "Aurora 7 #11" the poet emerges complete whole, teacher & self, talking to the world his world, face to face, completely out of the closet poetically so to speak, without losing poetic dignity as Tantrick Lama & Guru: "Here comes Chögyie/Chögyie's for all/Take Chögyie as yours/Chögyam says: lots of love!/I'm yours!"

I must say, that there is something healthy about the American idiom as it's been charmed into being by Williams, Kerouac, Creeley and others, a frankness of person & accuracy to thought-forms & speech that may've been unheard of in other cultures, a freestyle stick-your-neck-out mortal humor of the "Far West." When the Great East enters this body speech & mind there is a ravishing combination of Total Anarchy & Total Discipline.

Well, has the transition been made, by this poet, from Absolute Truth expressed thru symbols ("riding on the white horse of Dharmata")⋆ to Relative Truth nail'd down in devotional commitment to the American Ground he's set out to transvalue & conquer?— In the drama of this book, yes, the author Chögyam, with all his Vajra Perfections, is the drunk poet on his throne in the Rockies proclaiming "Chögyie is yours." What will Walt Whitman's expansive children do faced with such a Person?

Allen Ginsberg
Land O'Lakes, 1976
Boulder, 1983

⋆*Rain of Wisdom,* tr. by Nalanda Translation, Committee (Boulder & London: Shambhala Publications, 1980), p. 285, "The Spontaneous Song of the White Banner" by Chögyam Trungpa.

PREFACE

THUNDER AND OCEAN.

This simple book of poetry presents evidence of how the Tibetan mind can tune into the Western mind. There is nothing extraordinary about this; but the important fact is that East and West can meet together, contradicting Kipling's verse: "Oh, East is East and West is West and never the twain shall meet."

Upon my arrival in the West, I felt strongly that a meeting of the two minds—culturally, spiritually, metaphysically—could be realized by means of "first thought best thought," the uncontaminated first glimpse of one another. With natural skepticism as well as deep appreciation, I applied myself to examine Western wisdom and uncover the nature of occidental insight. I found that I had to immerse myself thoroughly in everything, from the doctrines of Western religion up to the way people tied their shoelaces. I was intensely curious to discover in all this where were the true heart and the true brain. And I was determined to find these matters out by personal experience, rather than by secondhand account.

When I was learning English in New Delhi, and attempting to read English literature, one day by chance I found in a magazine a simple and beautiful haiku. It may have been an advertisement for some Japanese merchandise or it may have been a piece of Zen literature, but I was impressed and encouraged that the simplicity of its thought could be expressed in the English language. On another occasion, I attended a poetry recitation sponsored by the American women's club, in conjunction with the American Embassy. I was very struck by the reading, which I recall included works by T.S. Eliot. This was not hymn, chant, mantra or prayer, but just natural language used as poetry. Afterwards, I told the young lady who gave the reading how much I appreciated it. She replied that she was a mere student, traveling in India. She was from Australia, but had been born and educated in Great Britain.

From my early childhood in Tibet, I was always fascinated with language. When I was thirteen, I managed to learn the dialect of the neighborhood where my guru lived, and even some of the natives thought I came from their own district. To me, the vowels and consonants contained tremendous power. By my late teens, I was quite freely able to write poetry, religious or otherwise. So poetic expression had already become natural for me before I left Tibet. Then, when I went from India to England, English became like a second language to me. I used to watch how people would hollow their mouths and purse their lips as they spoke, the way they hissed their *s*'s, the way they said the *d* in "daring," or the way they pronounced *f* as if it were a yogic breathing exercise. I was completely captivated by English pronunciation, and in particular, during my studies at Oxford, by the way the Oxonians spoke.

Poetry, linguistic expression and music are identical as far as I am concerned. Once I was taken to a college chapel by my dear friend Mr. John Driver to hear the St. Matthew Passion. This was such a great discovery, experiencing the tremendous heroism and spiritual passion in that atmosphere of sanctity, that I felt as though the occasion were my private feast. From the beauty of the music I gained further appreciation of the Western legacy. A Tibetan friend who also attended felt nothing of the kind. His reaction was that "we had three boring hours listening to the noise of tin cans, pigeons, and chickens getting their necks wrung." I felt so energized as we came out into the chill of the English night that my friend panicked and thought I was in danger of being converted to Christianity!

After Great Britain, coming to North America was an amazing and amusing fanfare. The way people spoke and behaved with each other was like being in the midst of ten thousand wild horses. Nevertheless, I developed a great respect for the Americans.

I have met many American poets. Some are like coral snakes; some are frolicking deer; some are ripe apples; some are German shepherds who jump to conclusions whenever a sound is heard; some are squirrels minding their own business; some are peacocks who would like to display themselves but their feathers are falling apart; some are parrots who have no language of their own but pretend to be translators; some are bookworms killing themselves by eating more books; some are like mountains, dignified but proclaiming occasional avalanches; some are like oceans, endless mind joining sky and earth; some are like birds, flying freely, not afraid to take a bird's-eye view of the world; some are like lions—trustworthy, sharp and kind. I have confronted, worked with, learned from, fought and fallen in love with these American poets. All in all, the buddhadharma could not have been proclaimed in America without their contribution in introducing dharmic terms and teachings.

In this book of poetry, some selections are traditional, written in Tibetan and then translated as faithfully as possible. Others were composed in English in a stream-of-consciousness style such as has been employed by American poets. Some were written out of delight, appreciating the manner of the English language itself. I hope this humble book of mine may serve to illustrate how the Eastern and Western minds can join together, how dharma can be propagated in the occidental world, and how the English language can develop as a vehicle for proclaiming the dharma throughout the world.

I would like to thank Allen Ginsberg for his introduction and deep friendship, and I would also like to thank all the poets in America who contributed to this book—either positively or negatively. As is said: a month cannot happen without new moon as well as full, light cannot shine without shadows. My profound gratitude to everyone.

This preface was written on the eighteenth day of the fourth month of the Water Pig Year by the drunken Tibetan poet.

With blessings,
Chögyam Trungpa

Fasnacloich
29 May 1983

EDITOR'S PREFACE

THE ONE HUNDRED AND EIGHT POEMS published here, roughly in chronological order, are selected from among over four hundred composed by Vajracarya the Venerable Chögyam Trungpa, Rinpoche, between 1968—two years before his emigration from Great Britain to America—and the present year (1983). The majority of these poems were composed directly in English. The rest were written in Tibetan and then translated into English by the author. These translations were subsequently reviewed and, to varying degrees, revised by the Nalanda Translation Committee.

Seventeen poems and songs by Ven. Trungpa Rinpoche, composed prior to 1970, were previously published in *Mudra* (Shambhala, 1972). Several of the early selections in the present volume date from the same period as *Mudra,* but none are repetitions. Four devotional songs translated from the Tibetan appear in *The Rain of Wisdom* (Shambhala, 1980), two of which are republished here. A number of other poems have previously appeared elsewhere in a variety of anthologies and journals, especially in *Garuda* and the *Vajradhatu Sun.*

A minimum of annotation has been supplied. For clarification of Buddhist terms, concepts and imagery, the reader is referred to Ven. Trungpa Rinpoche's numerous published writings as well as works by others on the Buddhist teachings. To assist the reader in identifying certain topical references encountered in the poems, the following brief guide to significant persons and events is offered.

Ven. Trungpa Rinpoche's childhood in Tibet, his rigorous training as a *tulku* or enlightened lineage holder in the Kagyü lineage of Tibetan Buddhism, and his perilous escape from Tibet following the Chinese takeover of 1959 are graphically described in his autobiography *Born in Tibet* (Shambhala, 1977). The Epilogue to the third edition of that work describes Ven. Trungpa Rinpoche's years in India, working with the Tibetan refugee community and encountering Western culture; in England, studying at Oxford; in Scotland, as spiritual director of the Samye Ling Tibetan Meditation Centre; and his work in North America up through the mid-seventies. The disruptive events that resulted in Ven. Trungpa Rinpoche's departure from Great Britain to America are alluded to in several of the early poems collected here.

A chance encounter between Ven. Trungpa Rinpoche and Allen Ginsberg on a Manhattan street in 1970 (Ginsberg "stole" Trungpa's taxicab for his fatigued father) was the origin of a lasting and significant poetic colleagueship that grew to include encounters and friendships with many other American poets, and which found institutional expression in the creation in 1974 of the Jack Kerouac School of Poetics as a founding department of the Naropa Institute in Boulder, Colorado.

Nineteen seventy-four also marked the first of three historic visits to North America by the "dharma king," His Holiness the Sixteenth Gyalwa Karmapa, head of the Karma Kagyü lineage of Tibetan Buddhism. Each of these visits, as well as the untimely death of the Karmapa in November 1981, occasioned poems in this volume.

A milestone in Ven. Trungpa Rinpoche's work of propagating buddhadharma in the West was his appointment in 1976 of an American-born disciple, Ösel Tendzin (Thomas Frederick Rich), as his Vajra Regent or dharma heir. A number of the poems celebrate, counsel or admonish this spiritual son. Others are addressed to the poet's blood son, Ösel Mukpo, or to students, friends, admirers or detractors. Ven. Trungpa Rinpoche makes regular use of the "occasional" poem, and this traditional and now much neglected form is well-represented in the present volume.

Many of the poems, even when not explicitly occasional, draw inspiration from events in the life of the two major institutions founded by Ven. Trungpa Rinpoche since his arrival in North America: Vajradhatu—an association of Buddhist meditation centers; and The Nalanda Foundation—a nonsectarian nonprofit educational foundation that includes the Naropa Institute. These events include the annual three-month Vajradhatu Seminary for seasoned Buddhist practitioners; the international Dharmadhatu Conferences at which executive committee members from the numerous local practice centers in North America and Europe convene; Naropa Institute seminars and graduation ceremonies; and many others.

A prominent source of imagery for the poems—as for much of Ven. Trungpa Rinpoche's teaching—is the tradition of the Kingdom of Shambhala, a Buddhist-inspired but also secular vision of enlightened society that underlies the Shambhala Training program.

The poems composed in Tibetan are in traditional meters, consisting mostly of seven- or nine-syllable lines. Also traditional is the interweaving of prose and poetry, similar to the Japanese technique used by Bashō and others. As for the poems composed directly in English, they were in almost every case dictated to a secretary, most of them to this editor. A short description of the process involved may serve to illuminate the context of the poems and to give some indication of their place in Ven. Trungpa Rinpoche's overall work:

At the end of a long day of scheduled business—administrative meetings, individual or group audiences, perhaps a visit to a fledgling business venture, followed in the evening by a public talk or a community ceremony—late into the evening or even in the early hours of morning, Ven. Trungpa Rinpoche, just when his loyal but weary attendants think they are about to be released, declares, "Let's write a poem." Pen and paper are made ready. Then, perhaps with a few moments of silent thought, more likely with no pause at all, he commences to dictate. The dictation is unhesitating, at a rate as fast and upon occasion faster (alas!) than the scribe can record. At the conclusion of dictation, Rinpoche asks, "Are there any problems?" This leads to a quick review of any unclear or grammatically inconsistent passages. Perhaps a few changes, such as bringing persons or tenses into agreement, are made, rarely anything of substance—though in the process Rinpoche himself may be inspired to interject a new couplet or stanza. Then a title—often a title and subtitle—are supplied by the poet, and the scribe is called upon to read the newborn poem, in a strong voice and with good enunciation, to the small audience which typically is present on these occasions. More often than not, further poems reiterating this sequence of events will follow over the course of another hour or two, or three.

In compiling the present volume, Ven. Trungpa Rinpoche has guided the overall shape and contents. The editors' work has consisted primarily of rectifying punctuation and line structure; decisions in these matters have necessarily been somewhat arbitrary on the editors' parts, but based on guidelines put forward over the years by the author.

Tibetan calligraphy for the facing-page bilingual selections was executed by Ven. Karma Thinley Rinpoche and by Lama Ugyen Shenpen, and their contribution is hereby gratefully acknowledged. The Vajra Regent Ösel Tendzin took time out of his busy schedule for a complete reading of the penultimate version of the manuscript, and his guidance is acknowledged with gratitude. A continuing and crucial contribution has been made by the Editorial Department of Vajradhatu, consisting of Carolyn Gimian, Editor-in-Chief; Sarah Levy; and Richard Roth. Mr. Roth in particular was instrumental in the later stages of the project. Of the numerous others who have worked over the years in recording, typing, editing and preserving the poems, only a portion can be acknowledged here: Beverley H. Webster, Connie Berman, Berkley McKeever, Donna Holm, Emily Hilburn, Helen Green, Sherap Kohn, Marvin Casper and John Baker. Particular recognition is also due to the Nalanda Translation Committee, and especially to its executive director Larry Mermelstein, for their work in translating or revising earlier translations of the Tibetan selections. The author in his own preface has already acknowledged Allen Ginsberg, without whose persistent encouragement and generosity neither the poems themselves nor this volume would have taken form as here presented. Finally, I would like to thank publisher Samuel Bercholz equally for his patience and his impatience in fostering and forwarding this undertaking.

The unique and precious opportunity provided to me, as to others, of working intimately with Ven. Trungpa Rinpoche is an incalculable gift and beyond the poor power of our gratitude to acknowledge. Through the blessings of his transcendent wisdom and compassion, may our slight efforts be transmuted into benefit for all beings.

David I. Rome

FIRST THOUGHT BEST THOUGHT
108 Poems

THE SPONTANEOUS SONG OF
ENTERING INTO THE BLESSINGS AND
PROFOUND SAMAYA OF THE
ONLY FATHER GURU

Shri Heruka, the unchanging vajra mind,
The primordial buddha, all-pervading, the protector of all,
Padma Trime, you are the lord, the embodiment of all the victorious
    ones.
You are always reflected in the clear mirror of my mind.

In the space of innate ground mahamudra,
The dance of the self-luminous vajra queen takes place,
And passion and aggression, the movements of the mind, become
    the wheel of wisdom;
What joy it is to see the great ultimate mandala!

The confidence of the unflinching youthful warrior flourishes,
Cutting the aortas of the degraded three lords of materialism
And dancing the sword dance of penetrating insight;
This is the blessing of my only father guru.

Inviting the rays of the waxing moon, Vajra Avalokiteshvara,
The tide of the ocean of compassion swells,
Your only son, Chökyi Gyatso, blossoms as a white lotus;
This is due to the limitless buddha activity of my guru.

In the vast space of mahashunyata, devoid of all expression,
The wings of simplicity and luminosity spread
As the snake-knot of conceptual mind uncoils in space;
Only father guru, I can never repay your kindness.

Alone, following the example of the youthful son of the victorious
    ones,
Riding the chariot of the limitless six paramitas,
Inviting infinite sentient beings as passengers,
Raising the banner of the magnificent bodhisattvas,
I continue as your heir, my only father guru.

Like a mountain, without the complexities of movement,
I meditate in the nature of the seven vajras,
Subjugating Rudra with the hundred rays of deva, mantra, and
    mudra,
Beating the victory drum of the great secret vajrayana,
I fulfill the wishes of my only father, the authentic guru.

In the sky of dharmadhatu, which exhausts the conventions of the nine
    yanas,
Gathering rainclouds thick with the blessings of the ultimate lineage,
Roaring the thunder of relentless crazy wisdom,
Bringing down the rain that cools the hot anguish of the dark age,
As I transform existence into a heavenly wheel of dharma,
Please, my only father, authentic guru, come as my guest.

2

STRAY DOG

Chögyam is merely a stray dog.
He wanders around the world,
Ocean or snow-peak mountain pass.
Chögyam will tread along as a stray dog
Without even thinking of his next meal.
He will seek friendship with birds and jackals
And any wild animals.

THE SONG OF THE WANDERER

The mood of sadness is inexhaustible;
Trying to end it would be
Like trying to reach the limits of space.
The feeling of longing is sharp and quick
Like an arrow shot by a skillful archer.

Across the sea in an Asian island
There are wild flowers of every kind.
These flowers are inseparable from the yogi's experience.
This is too realistic to be only a dream,
But if it is really happening
I must say it is rather amusing.

In the land of Bhutan
Where the mountains are clothed in mist
Young Chögyam is wandering like a stray dog.
In the hermitage of the Blue Rock Castle
A pregnant tigress is suckling her young.
There we found the nectar of the new age.

1968
Bhutan

4

Listen, listen

Listen, listen to the sound of the mind's own utterance,
Within the womb of the beauty of Autumn,
While the setting sun shows the red glory of her smile.
Hearing the bamboo flute which no one plays,
Listen to the reeds swaying in the breeze,
And the silent ripple's song.

The disciples debate,
But never reach the ripple's end.
The teacher's word that lies beyond the mind—
Listened to, it cannot be found,
And found, it still cannot be heard.

Whistling grasses of the Esk Valley

Whistling grasses of the Esk Valley,
So many incidents occur.
The image is the climate of this part of the country.
There comes a hailstorm—
Children, children, seek protection!
A mighty thunderbolt strikes to the ground.
It does not make any distinction between trustees and the spiritual
    leader.
Violent winds shake the Scots pine tree,
Copper beech and rhododendrons.
I said to myself,
You, most mighty of all, should have come three weeks earlier.
Here is the big storm.
Buckets of rain pour down.
The Esk river turns reddish in color,
Sweeps all the trees and branches away.
A mighty force invades our valley—
Fishes thrown up on the banks for the birds' delight.

Chögyam watches all this,
Wishing that I could be one of those fishes,
That this ruthless political current would throw me away.
Why wasn't I born an innocent fish
That could die in peace on the banks of the Esk?
If karma exists the weather will adjust.
I am not seeking revenge.
I am seeking peace
As one of those fish peacefully dead on the bank,
Its body a feast of its victory.

But I cannot help thinking they will say grace before the meal,
And will have a good cook
To make their evening feast enjoyable.

31 October 1969
Scotland

6

SONG

A railway station,
People busy, involved in their affairs.
A park keeper,
Enjoying cutting the flowers with his secateurs,
Pruning the roses.
This life is normal to some people.
But to people like us it is not normal at all.
So many things happen—
They are all part of life.

A battlefield,
Innocent people being killed.
I am sure we could change the course of the bullet—
Wars are not fought for hate,
But for pursuing further development.

I saw in my mind innocent Easter.
Young as he was his whole head had been exploded.
To whom could I tell such neglect and cruelty?
Where does it come from?

I say no more.

This is a lonely song.
I sing in a peaceful valley
Where the glittering frost ignites with the spark of sun.
This beauty does not satisfy me.
Come my friends, who has got heart?
That we may dance
And come into effect,
Into the perpetual time.

20 November 1969

In the north of the sky

In the north of the sky there is a great and dark cloud
Just about to release a hailstorm.
Mind, children,
Mind, young puppies and kittens,
That your heads are not injured.
Yet these hailstorms are merely pellets of ice.

There were hundreds of magicians
Who tried to prevent storm and hail.
In the course of time
All the ritual hats, altars and ritual garments
Have been blown away by the force of the hailstorms.

Here comes Chögyam disguised as a hailstorm.
No one can confront him.
It is too proud to say Chögyam is invincible,
But it is true to say he cannot be defeated.
Chögyam is a tiger with whiskers and a confident smile.
This is not a poem of pride
Nor of self-glorification:
But he is what he is.
He escaped from the jaw of the lion.

"Clear away," says the commander,
"You are standing on no-man's land.
We do not want to shoot innocent people."
We cannot alter the path of the shell.
Once the bomb is released it knows its duty;
It has to descend.
Chögyam knows the course of his action.

He could be described as a skillful pilot;
He can travel faster than sound,
Faster than thoughts.
He is like a sharp bamboo dagger
That can exterminate pterodactyls
Or fast moving boa constrictors.

I am not interested in playing games.
But what is a game?
It is a game when you shoot pheasants and deer.
You might say this is the game of the politicians,
Rather like the game of mah-jongg
Or that of chess.
Devoid of these games
I will sail straight through
Like a ship sailing through icebergs.
No one can change Chögyam's course,
His great odyssey.

The world waits,
Squirrels in the forest
And those of the moon
Listening in silence
Amidst gently moving clouds.
There is a force of silence
With energy
Which can never be interrupted.
With conviction and energy
I send my love to you.
I love you.

23 November 1969

GOODBYE AND WELCOME

"Goodbye"
"Welcome"
"Glad to meet you"
"How do you do"—
All this I hear
Echoing in the cave of social meeting,
And the echo goes on and on
Until it dies in the mountain depths,
Powerless to reflect.
But O World, O Universe,
My journey to the overseas continent needs no copyright,
For it has never been conducted in the same manner.
It is the fresh meeting of man,
The true meeting of living man.
It is the pilgrimage,
The great odyssey which I have never feared,
Since I have not hesitated to flow with the river's current.

With blessings and wisdom I write this poem,
As I am free once and for all
In the midst of friends who radiate true love.
Love to you all.

16 December 1969

9

Meteoric iron mountain

Meteoric iron mountain piercing to the sky,
With lightning and hailstorm clouds round about it.
There is so much energy where I live
Which feeds me.
There is no romantic mystique,
There is just a village boy
On a cold wet morning
Going to the farm
Fetching milk for the family.
Foolishness and wisdom
Grandeur and simplicity
Are all the same
Because they live on what they are.
There is no application for exotic wisdom,
Wisdom must communicate
To the men of now.
Dharma is the study of what is
And fulfills the understanding of what is here right now.
The ripple expands when you throw the pebble:
It is true, a fact.
That is the point of faith,
Of full conviction,
Which no one can defeat or challenge.

Please, readers,
Read it slowly
So you can feel
That depth of calmness as you read.
Love to you.
I am the Bodhisattva who will not abandon you,
In accordance with my vow.
Compassion to all.

17 December 1969

10

The Zen teacher

The Zen teacher hates the horse
But the horse carries him;
At the river both depend on the boat.

For crossing the mountains
It is better to carry a stick.

AMERICAN GOOD INTENTIONS

So violent in achieving nonviolence
A journey to the moon and the discovery of kundalini
Spiritual testimonials and presidential promises
Law and order and militant monasticism
Colorful gurus on sale at the A & P
Buddhologists
Rosicrucians
Masons
Zen profundity
Benevolent Protective Order of Elks
Electricity by the megawatts
Potential children discover potential parents
Virginia aristocrats
New York Jews
Mississippi is a meaningless noun
Idaho with its potatoes
Cape Kennedy with its moon
Washington, D.C., with its clean-cut
Chicago with its notorious Mafiosi
Telegraph Avenue sells Himalayan art in Berkeley
Canadian internationalism a cheap copy of the U.S.'s
A franchised Ugandan dictator
Black
Yellow
Crimson
Purple
All are primitive jokes
White cons black into grey
War is an opportune time to create peace
Nationwide respectability fails to include street-trained dogs

Oath of Allegiance violates a sense of humor
Yellow cabs roar through skyscraper canyons
Urban jackals patrol the streets crying red white and blue
Officials entertaining foreign dignitaries
Are busy apologizing for the presence of radical demonstrators

Wide as American inspiration
Profound as American patriotism
Protector of the free world
Praiseworthy
Questionable
Dignity is the object
God save America, our karmic sweet home.

May 1972

Dö-me sem (*Primordial Mind*)

12

FIRST THOUGHT

First thought is best
Then you compose
Composition's what you compose—
In terms of what?
What is *what*
And *what* might not be the best
That what could be best
That *what-was* was the only best
Why didn't you?
The first thought was the first what
That what was the best what
What might not be is heartbroken
Heart is your only security
What shall we do?
What shouldn't we do?
What did you say?
I forgot what I was just about to say
I was just about getting interested
In what you have to say
I'm glad that you want to tell me
What you want to say
What was it that you wanted to tell me?
Is *that* so
That you want to tell me what he'd like to tell me
That wouldn't be difficult
But she might hesitate
It is problematic
In my honesty to tell you
What I would like to tell you
Who do you think is kidding who?

I have no kids
You are the star of the world
I didn't take part in starving
Moon is good enough
So is the earth
And the water
I take refuge in the Buddha as an example
I take refuge in the Dharma as the path
I take refuge in the Sangha as the companionship
I am that which I I I I
And so forth.

May 1972

13

SAMSARA AND NIRVANA

A crow is black
Because the lotus is white.
Ants run fast
Because the elephant is slow.
Buddha was profound;
Sentient beings are confused.

22 May 1972

॥ །ཐོབ་པ་དང་ནོར་བུ།

ཤེ་མ་མྱུ་ཏོ་བའི་ག་སོ་སོ་ནི། །

ཊ་མས་མྱུ་ཏོ་མེ་ད་པའི་པ་ཀུན་འདུ། །

ཤེ་རས་གསོ་ནོ་ར་མ་ཀྱུར་བ། །

སྒོ་ནོ་ར་སྒྱུག་པ་ར་ཀྱུར་པ་འདུ། །

ག་ཞས་མ་མྱུ་ཏོ་བའི་སྒྲུན་པོ་ནི། །

ལ་ད་ཚོ་མེ་ད་པའི་ག་ཞོ་སྐྱུ་འདུ། །

སྒུན་པོ་ག་ཞས་པ་ར་ཀྱུར་པ་ནི། །

སུ་སྒྲོ་ཀྱལ་པོ་ར་ཀྱུར་པ་འདུ། །

སྒོ་ཊི་བ་དག་པོ་ར་ཀྱུར་པ་ནི། །

གསར་པ་ཧྗེའི་ཀྱལ་ཁ་ཐོབ་པ་འདུ། །

སྒོ་ཊི་བ་དག་པོ་ར་ཀྱུར་པ་ནི། །

མྱེ་ལ་མ་བཟང་པོ་སོ་ད་པ་འདུ། །

རེ་ར་འཇེས་སྒྲོ་གས་པོ་བཞུ་ད་པ་ནི། །

ར་ང་གི་མ་ཇ་ད་ད་ར་སྒྲོག་པ་འདུ། །

སྒྲོ་གས་པོ་གསར་པ་ཆེ་ད་པ་ནི། །

སྒུ་ག་ཞས་གསར་བ་ཚོ་མ་པ་འདུ། །

ཚོས་ཀྱམ་སྐྱན་དག་ཐྲི་བ་ནི། །

ཀྱལ་པོས་ད་མག་ཊེས་ཞེན་པ་འདུ། །

20

14

GAIN AND LOSS

He who has not experienced death
Is like an inexperienced father.
He who has not come to life after death
Is like a man suddenly struck dumb.
He who has never been wise
Is like a youth who has never been beautiful.
The stupid man who becomes wise
Is like a beggar who becomes king.
The dog who becomes master
Is like the victor in the revolution.
The master who becomes a dog
Is like a man who has awakened from a pleasant dream.
Meeting an old friend
Is like reading your own autobiography.
Finding a new friend
Is like composing music.
Chögyam writing a poem
Is like a king inspecting his soldiers.

22 May 1972

༄། ཟུར་ཟའི་ཡེ་ཤེ།

།སྐུ་གྲི་སོ་ཡེ་སྐྱང་རྟེ་བཤགས།
།མ་ཁས་པའི་མི་འཁྲུས་ཡིག་ཆས་བཏོན།
མ་ཟེམས་མ་འི་བཞིན་རས་དོམ་པས་ཀྲས།
དཔའ་བོ་འཇིགས་མ་ཞེས་པ་ཕུ།
འཁོར་བའི་ཚོས་ལ་གདུ་བོ་ནོ།
སྤུན་གྲགས་ཚན་ཆམས་འོན་པར་གྱུར།
བརྫ་བའི་ལག་པ་གྱ་མ་བྱས་གདུང་།
ཕྱི་ལ་བ་མར་མེ་འི་ནད་དུ་མ་ཆོངས།
བོང་བ་མེ་སྐྱོན་ཕོག་ནས་འགྲོ།
ནུ་བོ་ཆུང་བུ་ིི་འི་འཁོར་ལོས་ཀྱག
སྤུན་པོ་གསུང་བའབད་ཟབ་ཆེ་ག་ཝས།
གད་མོ་ཁོར་བའི་སྤུན་རག་མ་ཁན།
དྲུགས་ཀྱི་ཀྱ་བཟད་ཇེ་ཤུང་།

ཚོས་པ་ཆོས་བཞིན་སྐྱོད་པས་འཁོར།
ཆོས་མ་སྐྱོད་ན་འཁོར་མི་ཞེས།
སྡིག་ཆན་ཆོས་བཞིན་འཁོར་མ་ཤེས།
འཁོར་མ་ཤེས་པ་སྐྱེ་ཀྱིས་འཁོར།
ནས་ལ་འཁྱེར་ཀ་ལ་འཁྱེར་སྐྱོ་མ་པས་འཁོར།
རྫ་འཁོར་མེད་ན་ཀ་ལ་འཁྱེར་མེན།
ཆོས་ཀྱ་མ་འཁོར་བ་བསླས་པས་འཁོར།
འཁོར་ན་མེད་ན་ཆོས་ཀྱ་མ་མེད།

CYNICAL LETTER

Licking honey from a razor blade,
Eyes of the learned gouged out by books,
The beauty of maidens worn by display,
The warrior dead from not knowing fear—
It is ironical to see the dharma of samsara:
Celebrities deafened by fame,
The hand of the artist crippled by rheumatism.

The moth flew into the oil lamp,
The blind man walks with a torch,
The cripple runs in his wheelchair,
A fool's rhetoric is deep and learned,
The laughing poet
Has run out of breath and died.
The religious spin circles, in accordance with religion;
If they had not practiced their religion, they could not spin.
The sinner cannot spin according to religion;
He spins according to not knowing how to spin.
The yogis spin by practicing yoga;
If they don't have chakras to spin, they are not yogis.
Chögyam is spinning, watching the spinning/samsara;
If there is no samsara/spinning, there is no Chögyam.

22 May 1972

DIGNIFIED ROCKY MOUNTAIN

There is a big rocky mountain, like a dagger hoisted toward the sky, on which pine trees and long grasses grow. It is like a naked demon, standing erect wearing a bearskin. At the foot of this motion-less rocky mountain flows a river, dark blue in color. Around the mountain the breeze blows, peaceful and gently cooling. The sun is waiting to set. In the distant meadow, on the other side of the marsh, on the grassy hill, almost out of sight, the shepherds are gathering their flocks of sheep into the fold. The mood is relaxed but uncertain. There is an air of desire for friendly conversation. Should one rest one's mind by gazing at the rocky mountain? Or, gazing at the river, should one listen to its melody? Or, listening to the call of the shepherd, should one perhaps look off into the distance? It is uncertain.

> If the dignified mountain does not pierce the heavens,
> Who cares if the blue sky falls into the river?
> If the flock of sheep sleep peacefully in the fold,
> Who cares if there is no friend to talk to?
> Since thoughts, like feathers, are blown by the wind of hope
>   and fear,
> The dignified poet remains wherever he is.

26 May 1972

PHILOSOPHER FOOL

There is a famous snow mountain capped with mist, like a king wearing a crown. It is said that from this mountain one may see the North and South Poles simultaneously. This mountain is encircled by other awesome rocky snow mountains, like a king surrounded by his queen and ministers. At the foot of this range lies a valley famous as a retreat for meditators. The air is redolent with the fragrance of herbs and mountain freshness. Workers, toiling endlessly, have dreamed of visiting this place. In this peaceful and beautiful forest grow flowering willows, blossoming rhododendrons, beech, pines, and many wild flowers. There is a waterfall, like white silk scarves hanging. The sound of falling water is inviting.

Near the waterfall stands a simple stone house, uncluttered by ostentatious ornament. It blends easily into the rocky landscape. Inside, the pillars and beams are of cedar. In the front, a large window opens onto a porch. Blue smoke once lifted gently from the chimney and disappeared into the sky. Here lived a famous scholar. His room was completely lined with books. He enjoyed the beauty of nature and was competent in the fields of philosophy, art, medicine, and poetry. He spent all his time in taking long walks and in reading and writing. Occasionally, dwelling in retreat, he suppressed memories of work and struggle in his earlier life in the cities. He treated his servant–disciple in a fatherly manner, but with a certain measure of pride and disdain, which insured his obedience and efficiency. He instructed his disciple in all matters, from how to brew tea and cook food to the fine points of philosophy. His servant never spoke to him, for his time was taken up with listening to the scholar.

Once they took a walk, and his servant warned him that the bridge they were about to cross was unsafe. But the scholar would not listen. For an answer, the teacher said, "The scope of my vision is much greater than yours." As he trod on the bridge, it collapsed and he died in the turbulent river.

In the pure land of the beautiful snow ranges
Lived a learned man, a poisonous flower with venom–nectar.
The disease of pride turned him deaf and dumb.
On hearing a word of advice, he committed suicide.
A man foolishly wise is like a leper;
A wisely foolish man is like a baby learning to walk.
To ride the horse of knowledge, it is necessary to have a saddle.

27 May 1972

18

Does love kill anybody?

Does love kill anybody?
What is the sound of one hand clapping?
Love is not a burden, my dear!
Poetry is not a burden for the true poet.
The notion of "chain"
The notion of "blade"
Flowers
Honey
The moon
Chrysanthemums
Sweet smile
Teenager
College kids
Sharpened pencil
Incense sticks by the dozen
Red ribbons in your hair
Coca-Cola advertisements which speak of "action"
Sportsmanship
Skiing in the snow
A red pullover
Drinking cool beer
Be a sportsman in a unisex outfit
Sky-blue with red passion-stripes
Go-go person with wings on your sneakers
Intercontinental cosmopolitan sportsman getting into the love—
More poetry
More literature
Tokyo Cairo New Delhi Taj Mahal Paris
Blond hair of Oslo blond mule blond Pekingese—
Arabs brew good coffee,

But stabbing each other with a jewel-inlaid hack knife is another
    matter.
Love by telephone
Writing a love letter is creating a mistress
Bachelor creates mistress by making a date
Mind's duplicity
Run
Kick
Philosopher
Technocrats
Autocrats
Are bound by a unilateral declaration—
Money is no object.
What the wind sweeps,
What the fires burn,
I fall in love
Because love falls into me at home.
Rock is not loveable
But its not-loveableness is loveable.
Take a thistle to bed
And make love to it.

5 June 1972

19

A LETTER TO MARPA

Solid Marpa
Our father,
The message of the lineage:
You are the breadwinner.
Without your farm we would starve to death.
Fertilizing
Plowing
Sowing
Irrigating
Weeding
Harvesting;
Without your farm we are poverty-stricken.
Your stout body,
Sunburnt face;
Ordering Damema to serve beer for a break;
Evidence of the three journeys you made to India in you—
We sympathize with you for your son's death:
It was not the fault of the horse,
It was the seduction of the stirrup in which his foot was caught
As his head smashed into the boulders of conceptualization.
Yet you produced more sons:
Eagle-like Milarepa who dwells in the rocks,
Snow-lion-like Gampopa whose lair is in the Gampo hills,
Elephant-like Karmapas who majestically care for their young.
Tiger-like Chögyam roaming in foreign jungles.
As your lineage says, "The grandchildren are more accomplished
     than the parents."
Your garuda egg hatches
As the contagious energy of Mahamudra conquers the world.
We are the descendants of lions and garudas.

6 June 1972

ཕ་ལས་ཉིས་ཏེ་མ་ལ་བཙོང་།

ཞི་སར་ཐེབ་པ་གྲོགས་པོར་བྱིན།

རྒྱུན་མས་བཕོག་མ་རྣུས་པའི་ནོར།

དཀྱིལ་འཁོར་གྱི་བ་ཟེག་ཡིན།

མ་ཁས་པ་རང་མགོ་རྒྱས་བ་ན།

ཞིད་གི་ཤང་ཡང་འཛིན་པར་གྱུར།

སྤྱོབ་མ་ལོང་བའི་ཊུ་ཚོགས་རྣམས།

མཁས་པའི་དངུ་མ་ཐོང་བས་ཡིན།

གསར་དུ་བསྐྱེས་པའི་སྤྱོབ་དཔོན་དེ།

གསུང་བ་ཤད་བཙན་པོའི་བཀའ་ཁྲབ་པ།

ཉམས་མྱོང་ཅན་གྱི་སྤྱོབ་མ་ཆོས།

བཀའ་འདྲི་ཞབ་པོ་ཊེས་པས་ཡིན།

ཟེག་པོ་འདྲེན་པར་མཐོང་ནས་སུ།

ཕུས་ཕོག་འབུལ་བའི་བྱུན་དཅན།

གཡར་དུ་ཞོན་བཞིན་གཉི་དཁག་པས།

ད་ཡིས་གྱི་ལོག་ཁྲེར་བ་འདྲ།

20

APHORISMS

You bought it from your father, you sold it to your mother,
You shared the profit with friends;
Thieves can't steal this wealth—
Your family heirloom is arrogance.

When the scholar's head rots
His nose becomes deaf.
It's the fault of the blind students
Who fail to see his head.

The lecture of the newly appointed teacher
Sounds like a general's orders.
It's the fault of the senior students
For asking profound questions.

Mistaking a charlatan for a savior
And offering him one's life with blind faith
Is like falling asleep on a borrowed horse:
The horse will return to its owner.

The restless poet who composes
A verse in praise of mountain solitude
Is like a criminal turned judge
Writing a textbook on law.

The insight which transcends mind
And the mind which activates awareness
Are like a healthy youth
Who has good eyes and legs.

7 November 1972

21

THE NAMELESS CHILD

There is a mountain of gold. When the sun's rays strike it, it is irritating to look at. It is surrounded by red, green, yellow, orange, pink and liver-colored clouds, wafted gently by the wind. Around the mountain fly thousands of copper-winged birds with silver heads and iron beaks. A ruby sun rises in the East and a crystal moon sets in the West. The whole earth is covered with pearl-dust snow. Upon it a luminous child without a name instantaneously comes into being.

> The golden mountain is dignified, the sunlight is blazing red.
> Dreamlike clouds of many colors float across the sky.
> In the place where iron birds croak,
> The instantaneously born child can find no name.

Because he has no father, the child has no family line. Because he has no mother, he has never tasted milk. Because he has neither brother nor sister, he has no one to play with. Having no house to live in, he cannot find a crib. Since he has no nanny, he has never cried. There is no civilization, so he cannot find toys. Since there is no point of reference, he doesn't know a self. He has never heard spoken language, so he has never experienced fear.

The child walks in every direction, but does not come across anything. He sits down slowly on the ground. Nothing happens. The colorful world seems sometimes to exist and sometimes not. He gathers a handful of pearl dust and lets it trickle through his fingers. He gathers another handful and slowly takes it into his mouth. Hearing the pearl dust crunch between his teeth, he gazes at the ruby sun setting and the crystal moon rising. Suddenly, a whole galaxy of stars wondrously appears and he lies on his back to admire their patterns. The nameless child falls into a deep sleep, but has no dreams.

The child's world has no beginning or end.
To him, colors are neither beautiful nor ugly.
The child's nature has no preconceived notion of birth and death.
The golden mountain is solid and unchanging,
The ruby sun is all-pervading,
The crystal moon watches over millions of stars.
The child exists without preconceptions.

3 November 1972

22

THE MYTH OF FREEDOM

An intelligent and highly emotional young man, disliking the hustle and bustle of the city and the impositions of friends and relatives, decided to leave. He set out on foot and soon found himself crossing pleasant valleys and woods. He found a solitary and peaceful spot and decided to settle there. He enjoyed the sight of wild animals roaming freely, and flocks of birds.

> As the moonlight of peace and solitude spreads,
> Wild animals roam free and harmless.
> The wild flowers and trees are glamorous,
> The scent of herbs is pervasive.
> Who wouldn't take delight in this solitude, worthy to be praised
> by Brahma?

At times the young man dwelling in solitude is full of joy, at times he is afraid. Sometimes he has thoughts of the city and the years spent with his relatives and friends. Sometimes he feels uncomfortable at being in the mountain emptiness and becomes afraid that wild animals will attack him. He has ample supplies of food, but still he has the constant fear of running out. He has looked at the delightful landscape too long, and now it appears irritatingly monotonous. The tuneful song of the birds becomes mocking. He can't get to sleep at night, so he feels very tired during the day, and the boundary between waking experience and dream becomes fuzzy. Altogether, he suffers continually from paranoia and daydreams, and doesn't know what to do. He is imprisoned in his own projections.

> The external projection is empty of good and bad,
> The internal fixation of hope and fear imprisons.
> Truth and falsehood are at war.
> The simple-minded child is wounded by the arrow of confusion.

Sometimes he thinks of returning to the city and sometimes he thinks of hiding in the nearest village. He just wants to leave the desolate countryside. Finally, he ties his things into a bundle and goes back to the city. He meets his friends and relatives, but the fear he felt in his desolate retreat continues to haunt him. Sometimes he sees his friends and relatives as illusory maidens dancing, and sometimes as a threatening army. In the midst of such uncertainty, he wishes he could find a friend with whom to discuss the whole thing. But he doesn't know how to find a friend who is not an illusion. So the young man tries to find the boundary between illusion and reality.

When the endless illusory plot is all-pervading,
The folly of mind's limitless duplicity is uncovered.
By running away from friends you discover illusory friends.
Friends manifesting as enemies is the nature of illusion;
By projecting your duplicity on others you lose your own
  ground.
The friend who is not an illusory projection is found in
  yourself.

5 November 1972

36

23

HAIKU

The beginner in meditation
Resembles a hunting dog
Having a bad dream.

His parents are having tea
With his new girlfriend—
Like a general inspecting the troops.

Skiing in a red and blue outfit,
Drinking cold beer with a lovely smile—
I wonder if I'm one of them?

Coming home from work,
Still he hears the phone
Ringing in the office.

Gentle day's flower—
The hummingbird competes
With the stillness of the air.

7 November 1972

The red flag flies

The red flag flies above the Potala,
The people of Tibet are drowned in an ocean of blood;
A vampire army fills the mountains and plains,
But self-existing dignity never wanes.

10 November 1972

25

The sword of hatred

The sword of hatred is ornamented with the handle of invasion,
A red star has imprisoned the sun and moon,
The high snow-peaked mountains are cloaked in the darkness of a
    poisonous wind;
The peaceful valleys have been shattered by the sound of artillery.
But the dignity of the Tibetan people competes with the glory of the
    sky.

10 November 1972

ཀླུ་ཀྲུལ་བདེ་བར་བཀྲམ་པའི་སྤྲང་ལྕོངས་མེ་ཏོག་གཡུ་བཞིན་མཛེས་པས་བ་གྲུན ། །

ན་ཏུ་ཏུར་སྨྲ་སྒྲོགས་བཞིན་ཐ་ང་ཝིར་ཡལ་གཞི་སྒྱུ་གར་གཏམ་སྤྱང་བག་ཡར་ཉེར །

ཐག་དམར་དོད་ཚང་ཅན་གྱི་དཔ་རྗེ་ར་ལྷ་ཐེའི་དར་ཚ་རྫུར་གིས་བརྒྱོད་ལ་བསྒྱུ ། །

འགྲོག་པའི་ཕྱུགས་སྐྱ་ནག་པོར་སྒྲ་ཁྱིམ་རྗེ་ནས་དཔ་ལ་སྟོན་པོ་དཔལ་ཉལ་ཡང་ །

སྦ་མཚད་མ་སྒྱིན་དུ་ཕེབས་པའི་ཌ་དང་དུང་གི་རོལ་མོས་གྲགས་ཚ་རྒྱ་ནས་སྒྲོག་ས །

ས་མཐོ་བོད་ཀྱི་གངས་ཅ་ན་ཡལ་སྤྱོངས་མཐལ་བས་དགའ་སྐྱིའི་ནོ་སྨ་ལུག་ཏུ་མེར །

རྒྱ་བོ་སྤོང་ཐག་བན་ལ་ཀྱང་ས་མཐབ་མ་ཚེར་རྒྱ་སྐྱེའི་གཏམ་བཆར་ཏན་པས་སུན །

ཐག་རོར་འགྲོག་པའི་སྒྲ་ནག་མཐོང་བར་འདུམས་གཏར་ནས་བསྒྱོད་ཀྱང་སྤྱེན་རྒྱ་མེར །

ཏེ་རོར་རལ་དུན་ཆེ་བས་རྩ་རྒྱ་མེ་ཞིང་འརྫོམ་སར་སྤོད་གྱུར་བརྒྱབ་ན་བསམ ། །

SILK ROAD

A herd of sheep roam on the meadows ornamented with turquoise
    flowers;
The crow caws on the pine branch, conversing easily with the magpie.
Flags flutter on a cairn, on a red rock peak where vultures nest.
From a black tent amidst dark old yak folds smoke rises gently,
And the conches and drums of invited lamas echo in the distance—
Irrepressibly happy and sad to see the highlands of the snow land
    Tibet.

Traveling, listening to the whistling wind, crossing thousands of
    ridges but still not seeing the end of the earth;
Irritated by the gossip of the brooks, crossing thousands of rivers but
    still not reaching the end of the sky;
Never reaching the goal of the nomad's black tent in the distance—
It is too tiring for the horses and mules: better to pitch our tent
    where pasture, water and firewood are plentiful.

10 November 1972

TIBETAN PILGRIM

On the right, a mountain with juniper trees—at its foot a farmhouse topped with white prayer flags—is like a minister on a tigerskin seat.
On the left, a mountain covered with tamarisk trees—at its foot a farm filled with beautiful green wheat and barley—is like a queen on a silken throne.
Straight ahead, a rocky mountain rises above a monastery with glittering gold roofs like a king on a throne of gold.
An old pilgrim feasts his eyes on the richness of some merchant's camp, and patiently continues towards Lhasa.

10 November 1972

TRANS WORLD AIR

On perfecting the Sky Dance
Naropa wore out Doctrine
Metal mirror polished now
Syllable *Ah*'s image shines
Young moon searches out a Love
Hearing raven croak caw caw
Snowy mountain's song echoes
Raising dusty golden mists—
Better drop your iron pants.

29 October 1973

*Translated from the Tibetan by the
author and Allen Ginsberg*

29

A flower is always happy

A flower is always happy because it is beautiful
Bees sing their song of loneliness and weep
A waterfall is busy hurrying to the ocean
A poet is blown by the wind.

A friend without inside or outside
And a rock that is not happy or sad
Are watching the winter crescent moon
Suffering from the bitter wind.

2 February 1974

TRUE TANTRA GROUPIE

Sunset or sunrise in the Tantra Group—
The wicked people with pocket money
Are supposed to be truly dangerous.

Students of Vajrayana watching the glow of fire
Toasting their emotions
Might happen to eat them
With a thin spread of butter flavored with marmalade.

It is good that the fire is burning
That the water is flowing,
Stars in the galaxies are in their appropriate places.
The universe is loveable
To the extent that simultaneous orgasm can be shared.

Fire is red
Sky is blue
Grass is green—
Things as they are.
But they speak an unspeakable utterance:
That they have the right to complain.

Fire is red
Sky is blue
Grass is green
Fire is red
Sky is blue
Grass is green
Fire is red

Sky is blue
Grass is green

Who said that . . .

5 July 1974

GLORIOUS BHAGAVAD-GHETTO

Hawk is silly
Because of its hawkishness,
Good is bad
Because of its goodishness.
Bad is so good
Because of its bluntness.
Raven vulture lizard
A monk a nun
A dog a cat
Venerable mosquito
Sick frog
Healthy guinea pig
Giant grain of sand—
They all speak a mutual language:
Who we are
What we are
Maybe we are
The neighbors might know about us.
Do the neighbors know the Tantra?
What is Tantra?
Is black black?

Thanks be to the wise or the stupid,
Mrs. Jones
Mr. McLean.
Glory be to the rain
That brought down
Concentrated pollution
On the roof of my car
In the parking lot.

5 July 1974

TAIL OF THE TIGER

Darkness is good
With an incense stick burning,
Herbert speaks good language
Which becomes onomatopoeic,
Jews Jew
Because of Gentiles,
Thunder is good
It knows the mountains,
Food is bad for you
It makes you eat more,
Magic is contagious
Because there is none.
What is magic?
What isn't magic?
Is food shelter?
Or is shelter food?
The magicians are magpies,
A tiger is a poodle,
Having a tail is equal to a stiff upper lip,
Giant is dwarf—
Have a baby sitter!
Don't tread on the tail of a flea.

5 July 1974

NAROPA INSTITUTE, 1974

Long live the longest one
But we should be kind to the short ones
Flea on the Empire State Building
Mosquito in the Taj Mahal
Eiffel Tower like a growth on your thumb
The world is good!
But bad in many ways
On the other hand
Bad and good makes the world feel
Not so good
But at the same time
It makes it feel good
It's a checkerboard:
Good is bad
Bad is good
Goodbad! is good
Goodbad! is bad
Badgoodgood
Goodbadbad
Goodie is baddie
In the realm of
Goodgoodgood
At the same time
Badbadbad
If we take a cross-section
Badgood badgood
On the other hand
Goodbad goodbad
He is goodly bad
Therefore she could not be

She is badly good
Therefore he could not be
Mutually they are
Goodly bad badly good
Therefore they could be
Because of it
Bad is good
Bad is good
Bad is good
We are at a loss
Lost is good
Lost isn't good
Facts are figures
Figures are facts
Figurefacts figurefacts figurefacts
Facts are no figures
Figures no facts
John is not Mary
Mary is not John
John Mary John Mary John Mary
Oliver
Olivia
Teeth and tongue
Teeth can't be cooked
But tongue is delicious for a meal
Facts are not figures
But figures are facts
Computer is good
Because
Sun!
Moon!
Star!
Greenery!
Blue flower!
Honey!

Woodpecker!
Railroad!
Lotus pond Marvin Casper
Smile of dark-haired girl
Seduction of the blond
Blond moth
Pekingese pony
Graceful ant
Cockroaches in a New York apartment
Eiffel Tower
Empire State Building
Guards with handsome uniforms
Policeman blowing whistle musically
Ginsberg being pedantic
Joshua Zim in New Mexico
New New New
New New New
New England
New Mexico
Blacks don't get their privilege
Flying helicopter with cameramen
Honeymoon
Inspired glamorous youth
Wants to be made love to
Silk scarf
Nouveau riche
Good to be with
Jews or Gentiles
Are no longer the question
In the realm of youthful exuberance
Skiing in the mountains
Metaphysical debate
Glorious to be the dogshit in Brooklyn
Glorious to be in the glaciers of the Grand Tetons
Halvah is good to eat

Cheesecake is questionable
May they both be blessings on us
Facts and figures no longer important
January could afford to affront
February it's subordinate
March felt youthful
April is adolescent
Grass is green
Fire is ember
Turquoise is black
From the view of coral
World is good
Good is world
Bad is goodworld
Goodworld is bad
Let us bring
Venus
Glorious to be Ram Dass
When he sweats
With beads of perspiration in his hair.

Duncan Campbell
The moderator
Hot and cold
In moderation
Bewildered Baker
Overcooked Green
Open Secret oven
Glory be to them
While Chögyie and Dassie
Are cooking
Sweetsour curry rockBoulder
Glorious to be
Glorious to be
Glorious to be

Mining town
RockBoulder
Boulderrock
Good living in bhakti
So-called.
GOOD
BAD
BAD
GOOD
Bhakti
Shopper
Realism
Dilettante
Grasshopper
Devoted moth
Confused ant
Spiritual materialism
Syringe
Good grass
Fancy bread
Bhakti provocation
In the name of goodness
Complementary speech
In the name of Trungpa
Everything is good
Ram Dass is cult
In spite of the Baba
Square is round
Rock is water
Fire is tree
Impregnation is abortion
So unpleasant
Embarrassment of Ram Dass
Cutting through is love-and-lighty
Failure is complement

The world of goodness is full of fleas
Glorious to be the inspired true-believer
Hurricane!
Storm!
Thunderstorm!
Redandwhite redandwhite
RedAndWhite
REDANDWHITE
True blue of dharmakaya
Is the only solution,
Devoid of Jacob Needleman.

12 July 1974
Boulder, Colorado

34

PEMA YUMTSO

Gayle Beth
She is not certain
Seagulls
Moth
Honeymooners
Ring of her dead lover
Bees
Wasp
Wise owl
Clark Kent
Yeshiva
Black and white
Flamingos asleep on one leg
Giraffes are not Jews
Zebra likes bucking people
Glory be to Gayle
She's such a nice girl
Only if . . .
She's such a nice girl
Only if . . .
Only if . . .
If . . .
If . . .
She is truly what she claims
She is Mona Lisa
She isn't Mona Lisa
Is she?
Or isn't she?
If she sleeps on one leg like flamingo
She is

But then she's not giraffe
Zebra
Is she a lioness
A tigress?
Maybe she is
She seems to be palm tree
She is white raven
She is musician
Dancing on the strings of piano
She's a little gypsy girl
She's cute
She's powerful
She's the lily of the hidden valley
She's not secular
She's sacred
She's holy
She's immaculate
She's complainatory
She is her
She is blue
She's white
She's turquoise lake
She is what she is
She's angry woman
She's kind woman
She deserves what she is
Oh! she
Oh! she
She is Oh! she
Oh! she
Truth of the matter is
Just between us
She *is* tiger lily.

1 August 1974

35

TO BRITAIN'S HEALTH

Such sharpness
Such honesty
The world is made of truth and lie
Truth of deception
Who buys that?
Jigsaw puzzle is true
Cyclops doesn't see double-vision
World's sportsman
World's prettiest girl
Demanded by mankind of the world
Proud woman
Sharpened pencil
Peacock with dots
Hallucinogenic drugs
Golden Syrup
In the name of Her Majesty the Queen
Hollow cock
Rotten wood
Cathy McCullough at the campfire
I told you
You told me
I'm sorry I forgot
I wasn't paid for this
Humorous Jack Elias
Bob Halpern as jewel merchant
Tile of Mexico
Let us have a bullfight
Sword of prajna
Impeachment of the Buddha
Holy Dalai Lama

Quarterhorse
Mustang
Stallion
Honorable discharge
English saddle
Smell of good leather
Glory be to our Queen
Long live the Elizabeth the Second
My Queen
Towards whom I feel integrity
Long live the Queen
Stiff upper lips
Pleasing British leather saddle
Equitation
Diana Judith
Union Jack
Red white and blue
Glory be to Elizabeth the Second
The rushes of Scotland
Swamps of Northumberland
The dimples of the Lake District
Plains of Salisbury
White chalky shores of Dover and Devonshire—
There is something nice about our Kingdom
Glory be to Diana and her English nose
Foggy London
Confident boys
Union Jack flying
In the midst of traffic in Piccadilly
Still majestically bearing the symbol of St. George
And St. Andrew
St. Patrick
My second home
Glory be to the thistles, clover
And the royal rose

Cockney accent
The Liverpool accent
The Midlander's
The Welsh, Scottish
And the Irish
Such rich people
Enjoying the bank holiday at Blackpool—
May the Kingdom last long
May the Kingdom last long free from the Tory
The Labor
The Liberal
May Her Majesty ride on a powerful white horse
With her banner fluttering in the winds of English country power.

1 August 1974

SUPPLICATION TO THE EMPEROR

You are a rock
You are our foundation
You can cause a landslide
You can shake the earth
You are all the elements
You burn
You quench thirst
You sustain
You are the creator of turbulent fresh air
You sit like a mountain
The world is your throne
The world is helpless
You and your Kagyü lineage
Are the only living monarchs on earth.

Inter-cosmopolitan politics
International Ballistic Missile
Internal Revenue Service for rich hippie spiritual shoppers—
In the Age of Darkness
Your multiple all-pervasive macro-precision dharma-insight is so
    penetrating:
Amidst a flock of black sheep
A flock of black pigeons
A depressed herd of buffaloes
Shaggy polar bears munching vegetables
Black cloud hovering above polluted cities
Aluminum-rim black leather executive chairs
Nouveau-riche articulation getting into the silk and satin world
Ex-Catholics reentering because of the promise of the Mother Church
Sleepy Jews learning to play the Kabbalah puzzle

Hocus-pocus Hindus trying their best in the Armenian evangelical
      jinglebell
Tea parties' old den of Theosophy filled with chatter of the new
      Messiah
Oakwood-paneled meeting halls with deadly pamphlets advertising
      "That" or "This" trip in their elegant language:
This dungeon of dark tunnels where millions are trapped
Comparing their entrapments as better than others'.

O Dawn of Karmapa
Are you Avalokiteshvara?
If
Are
Are you
You are
So you
You must be
Come forth
The Dawn of Karmapa
The only living monarch on earth
Be kind to us
We wait for your lion's roar
Tiger's claw
Gentle smile
Ostentatious display of your presence.

You did
You will do
You are doing it
So do it
O Dawn of Karmapa.

9 September 1974
Tail of the Tiger
Barnet, Vermont

LITERAL MATHEMATICS

Zero is nothing
One is bold
Two is loneliness
Three is the other
Four is the peacemaker
Five is a group
Six is the parliament
Seven is a happy conclusion
Eight is security
Nine is trooping
Ten is convenient
Eleven is agitation
Twelve is helpless
Thirteen is a threat
Fourteen is a land speculator
Fifteen is a market researcher
Sixteen is the desperate
Seventeen is a troubleshooter for the ecologist
Eighteen is a silk merchant
Nineteen is a junior executive
Twenty is sportsmanship
Twenty-one is a Jewish banker—
But zero is one in the realm of oneness
Oneness is one in the realm of zeroness
Two is sixteen in the realm of eighteen
Twenty-one is glorious after the teething of the three
Sixteen is five nobody knows who they are
Seven is ten in the realm of coins
Nine is nineteen because of sharp corners
Three is eight you have chosen a bad tailor

Four is fourteen the grammar school is inadequate
Twenty is eighteen need for equitation lesson
Eleven is fifteen bad Christmas gift
Twelve is seventeen a carrot is not a radish
Thirteen is thirteen odd man out
Glory be to the six, good table manners.
Jam jar
Honey pot ·
Lemon sherbet
Who's kidding whom?
Kids are kite
Kites fly
Kids stumble
In the glorious desert mole-hole.
Life as it was.
Could life be?
I mean that way?
Do you really?
But zero is what?
Well . . . well, zero is.
Glory be to those who have missed aeroplane connections—
Fly United.

9 September 1974

One Way

Way one

Flea bite

Lion's roar

SHASTA ROAD

Rationalists have found that there is a bird in the sky.
Experimentalists say maybe this bird is a kite.
Donkeys have their way to be stubborn.
People from a Cossack town have their particular food.
Butterflies and bats have differences in their language.
Practitioners are fascinated by their practice,
Practitioners painfully experiencing their practice debating the reality
    of Timbuktu.
Million stones and trillions space are one in the area of mutual pain.
Gooseberry and chicken feet are one in the realm of totality.
Jungle kid and ocean crocodile are rebellious in the realm of mutual
    interest.
Highfaluted holiness depressed politician burning hot pliers
Are in the same realm as barking Pekingese at Madame Chang's
    apartment.
Max King and Patricia King and Martha Washington who knows,
Thistles poison oak grasshoppers made into juice,
Bushmen's Ph.D. Siamese cat eating frog eyes.
Prostrations are premature to give to the adolescent student.
Pinetree Doves Coralrock Porcupine Pippi Porky Poodle Pissmen
    are in the realm of polarities.
Glory be to tonight's poet.
Who's who? What's what? Nobody knows.
But everybody knows,
Including our kind neighbor who would never harm a flea,
But willing to cut your throat.

1 February 1975

40

Palm is

Palm is.
It may be small, but includes the universe:
Fortune-tellers make a living out of it;
Flamingos sleep on it;
Mothers slap their children;
It's for begging, giving;
When thinkers don't have thoughts, they rest their foreheads;
Trees that have palms invite holiday-makers.
Can a jackal read a palm?
Maybe S.C. can read—
But is S.C. a jackal?
S.C. is tricky,
But jackals are perky, with long throbbing howls;
Maybe they read their palms in the cold wintry night
In the aspen grove.
The Lord of Death supposedly reads palms,
To see through your life's work:
The good man
The wicked
Banker
Priest—
How many infants got slapped with a palm,
How much dough we molded with our palms,
How many directors clapped their palms on the table
Shouting, "Let's do it!"
I wonder whether Miss Bishop has used her palms in her life?
The palms of the night,
To write poem of palm.
Flamingos
Flamingos' mothers

S.C.
Fortune-tellers.

The earth is a big palm,
So is the sky;
Jointly they make the four seasons.
By mistake, cities grow up between their palms,
A vein of highways begins to grow,
There's no room to breathe—
People call it pollution.
I wonder what it's like to be the palm of the universe.
The stars and moons,
Saturn and Jupiter,
Mars and Venus,
Twinkle between two palms.
By fault of the palms being too tight,
Sometimes various comets escape
Creating cosmic fart:
The world of fart and palms.
Goodnight, jackal!

25 February 1975

41

BURDENSOME

The best minds of my generation are idiots,
They have such idiot compassion.
The world of charity is turned into chicken-foot,
The castles of diamond bought and sold for tourism—
Only, if only they . . .
Oh, forget it.
What is the use of synchronizing?
Raccoons are pure animals, they wash their food.
Beavers are clever animals, they build their dams.
Hot cross bun is for Easter.
Men who care for themselves turn into heroes
Walking on cloud—but are not dreamers—
But performing a miracle.
Distant flute makes you happy and sad—
Only for the shepherds.
Long lines of generations are hard workers.
Glory be to the blade of grass
That carries heavy frost
Turning into dew drop.

25 February 1975

TSÖNDRÜ NAMKHA

In the land of promises
One flea bite occurred.
In the midst of continental hoo-ha
One bubble occurred in a tall lager-and-lime glass.
Midst a spacious sand dune
Sand swarmed.
Lover with sweat.
Primordial egg dropped from the sky
And hit Genghis Khan's head
In the middle of the Gobi Desert.
Horny camels huffed and puffed to the nearest water.
Desert seagulls pushing their trips to gain another food.
Suzanne with her jellyfish
Volleyed back and forth by badminton rackets—
Oh this desert is so dusty
One never gains an inch
Not a drip of water
So sunny
Almost thirsty
Very thirsty
Fabulously thirsty
Terribly—
Oh it's killing me
This desert this sand
Preventing me from making love
Preventing me from eating delicious supper
With all-pervasive crunch of sand.
I wish I could go to the mountains
Eat snowflakes
Feel the cool breeze—

I wouldn't mind chewing icicles
Making the delicious cracking sound
As I step on the prematurely frozen pond,
Making the satisfying sound of deep hollowness
As I step on the well-matured frozen pond,
The undoubtedly solid and secure sound
On a fully-matured frozen pond.
Suzanne would love that,
Because she is the punisher in the desert
And she is the companion
When we skate across this large fully frozen pond.
Let's fly across the ice
Let's beat the drum of our hearts
Let's blow the bagpipe of our lungs
Let's jingle the bells of icicles
Let's be cool and crispy—
Suzanne, join us!
What is gained in the hot deserty wretched sweaty claustrophobic
    sandy skull-crunching dusty world of Gobi?
Who cares?
Come to the mountains, Suzanne,
O Suzanne!

March 1975

PEMA SEMMA

How small can you be?
So tiny that you can't even talk or think.
How big can you be?
So big that you can't think or talk.
Desert hounds are said to be tough
But, looking at their own ancestral skulls,
They could become painfully wretched.
Come, Come, said the young woman,
Come with me to the mountains
Where the heathers, rhododendrons, tamarisks and snowflakes grow.
Her hair fluttered by the cool mountain air
Which is so fresh,
Her lips and eyelids quivering at the freshness she experiences,
Sunbeam reflecting on the side of her face
Portrays a lady of life.
As she turns her head
From the little irritation of long flowing hair
She says, Mmmm.
But on the other hand she is somewhat perturbed;
Not knowing whether she is glamorous or ugly,
Begging for confirmations right and left,
Still listening to the distant flute of her past present future.
Is she wretched?
Is she fabulous?
Thundering heartbeat in her chest,
Riding the horse of jealousy at a million miles a minute—
Could someone fall in love with her?
Could she be the world's monumental femininity?
Is she the possible hag
Who eats living chrysanthemums or dead bees?

Winding highway to the Continental Divide,
Snake coiling for its own purpose,
Tortoise carrying heavy-duty shell with meaningful walk,
Red silk rustled,
Hearty blue-blood aristocracy
With its blue ribbon blown in the wind
From the palace window—
Is this such a woman as deserves a coronation ceremony attended by
    the galaxies, the stars and the world of yes and no?
Is she such a woman as is never hampered by a dirty, greasy,
    bullfighter, manslaughtering, unworthy man?
I wonder whether she has tasted her blood
Or her nectar.
Glory be to our Queen!
Lust is for everybody, by the gallons;
Envy is for one, who picks and chooses
Like a woodpecker digging after one worm.

However, everybody's a lover—
Let's celebrate in love!

7 March 1975

DYING LAUGHING

It is ironic that the pigeon got run over by a car.
It is sad that the M.C.P. people got insulted.
What's wrong with you is that you talk too much—
Or, for that matter, think.
Yesterday was a glorious day
Today is reasonable but a bit chilly.
Boomslangs never made friends with man,
But boa constrictors swallowed a church
And assumed its shape.
Joshua Zim appreciates highlights,
Or for that matter deep throat.
Flip a coin!
Take a chance!
What is the worth of all these thoughts?
A mustache is not worth it
If there is no mustacher.
On the whole, it's a gigantic black hole
Where things come and go in and out,
Sometimes cheap sometimes extravagant.
The world is a big mind
Which reacts to all conclusions.
Scattered thoughts are the best you can do.
Let the mercury jump on a drummer's drum
Breaking and gathering—
What's wrong with you is
You think too much,
Talk;
So don't talk
Or think;
Or, not talk first,

Then don't think;
Or, don't think first,
Then talk.
But finally we find non-talker, thinker;
Non-thinker, talker.
Let's forget about it all—
Om Shanti
Shhh
But don't . . .

Do it all anyway!
Let's do it completely!
That the whole universe could be exasperated
And die laughing!

7 March 1975

45

KÜNGA GARMA

Jalapeños are good to eat
Antelope has slanted eyes
There comes a rocket
Alice is magnificent
She's courageous
Fun-fair
Jalapeños seem to be good
In the midst of your surroundings
Biting
Hot
Tongue subjugator
Throat warmer
Alligatorial bite
Crocodillian nastiness
Oh Jalapeño
Montezuma's revenge
Lips of rectum may suffer from too much jalapeño
The next day.
A peacock has feathers
A tortoise has a shell
David Rome has a mustache
Gem business
How ironical the whole thing
The Star of David shines
In the midst of Mermelstein parental warmth
Action speaks louder than word.

Jade rock resides majestically
With a silk scarf of misty cloud wrapped around its neck,
Overhung by haunted pine trees

Pretending they are old hags
Welcoming guests who appreciate the view.
Acting as sages,
Wise frogs leap about in the atmosphere of humid rainy misty dim
    stove burning with an inner glow
While the ethnic mothers cook their porridge
With rustic smile.
Turtles walk slowly but surely in the midst of dimples of footprints
Which turn into puddles.
Tibetan sad-happy flute plays in the distance
While the roaring engines of jets resound overhead.
In the grove of maple trees
Where the bees cannot exist
Primrose, sagebrush, tamarisk hedges are growing magnificently,
Utterly competing with arrogant pampas grass shoots.

Who cares?
How cares?—
In the midst of jalapeño dumpling
Bitten by Alice's white teeth,
Which are lubricated with feminine saliva
And gentle touch.
The swelling of her femininity,
Acting as fabulous flexible rock,
Could be swayed by wind as if a tree.
No one has seen a dancing rock,
Powerful tree,
Punctuated by occasional freckles
On her old-aged motherly face
Which still remains magnificently youthful as a teenager.

Cuckoos and cockroaches speak different languages,
As Alice does.
Kung fu masters are subjugated by the beauty of Holiday Inn
In its magnificent funky service.

America has grown old
But still is getting younger,
Thanks to the presidential resignation of Nixon's scream
And hush hush that goes with it.
Another Star of David is jalapeño.
In midst of donkey's dung pussy cat is killed
Because of its Ginsberg resentment
To the Rockefellerian manipulation.
Arabs produce good coffee
With a dash of oil in it—
But nobody is comparable to the Alice in Wonderland's jalapeño
    trip.
Glory be to the would-be last monarch,
Prince Charles,
Who has no idea of jalapeño
Or our Alice.

March 1975

Gyal jö (*Victory Cry*)

1111 PEARL STREET
VICTORY CHATTER

As an old soldier
Watching the territory:
Flags go up and down
Where the soldiers gather;
Hearing distant archery contests;
Horses are unsaddled in the meadow;
Flute of a soldier who is in love;
Listening to the creaking of the cannon swayed in the wind.
The sound of the flute fades away;
The banner of victory is fluttered by the breeze;
Rustling of armor takes place constantly.
Occasional smell of horse dung,
Occasional cheerful chatter of the armed force—
I bide in the tent, the general,
Listening to the occasional grasshopper's leap:
How grateful to be a soldier.
Ah! storm rises,
Gold-black cloud in the southern quarter—
I can hear the flag fluttered violently by the wind.
A thought occurs to me:
"Somebody's getting out of the administration."
And another:
The memory of a whistling arrow on the battlefield
And the high-pitched echo of swift swordsmanship.
A thought occurs to me:
"Somebody's getting into business,"
As the horses begin to neigh—
They are ready for tomorrow's battle:
"Somebody's going to teach philosophy tomorrow

And get out of the administration at the end of the week."
The cloud from the south moves close to the center of the sky,
Dark with wrath.
We hear resounding deep thunder.
The warriors' fight must go on—
Vigor and bravery
Sharp sword
Well-cared-for bows and wrestling armor
Are our only resources.
Frontier warfare is sad and happy,
It is romantic and treacherous.
Oh! How I feel that I am a good soldier,
A good general,
Listening to the rustling of armor
Where the white tents are blown by the wind.
We are sharpening our swords and our arrowheads.
How romantic to be fighters
Conquering the American plains!
Good luck to Boulder
Rock
The Rocky Mountains
The pine trees—
Full of fantastic battlegrounds.
The kingdom rests at eleven and eleven.
It is good to fight,
It is good to know that victory is,
It is good that I alone can wage this particular warfare.
Sharpened sword
Arrowheads
I fight in the old fashion.

2 July 1975
Boulder, Colorado

WAIT AND THINK

Wounded son—
How sad.
Never expected this.
Oily seagulls
Crippled jackal
Complaining flower—
Very sad.
Is it?
Is it?
Is it?
Maybe a couple of doughnuts might cure
Or, for that matter, wine that is turning into vinegar.
Little flowers
Snow drops
Early bird—
Hopefully gentle breeze will turn into hurricane.
That might be somebody's wild guess.
William Burroughs' rhetoric
Single-minded
Street dogs
Thieving dogs—
Oh how fantastic this world.
Julius Caesar never made it.
Suns and moons have their problems,
The galaxies of stars have their problems among them.
Mysterious world sad and happy:
The problem is that we are too serious.
Gurdjieffian literal thinking
Theosophical secrecy
Maroon car

Defective door
Glorious in the name of one-upmanship.

Does His Holiness sneeze?
Does His Holiness cough?
If he does,
Who doesn't?
If he doesn't,
Who does?
Truth of the matter is
We are a gigantic spider
Constantly weaving webs
But never giving birth.
Who is not brave enough to swallow the sun
Eat the earth
Bathe with the galaxies?
Let us join this feast
Free from orgy and ritual.
Hallelujah!

4 July 1975

MISSING THE POINT

Brain hemorrhage
Sick pigeon
Trust in the heart
Good soldier
Neat girl in the cosmic whorehouse—
Our minds becoming bigger and smaller
As if they were Lynn's mustache
Which gets bigger and smaller as he talks.
Stalagmite stalactite
Mutual love affair—
Today I rose relatively early.
My thoughts are constant
Like a leak in an old castle
Plop plop plop ploo plop.
Things go on—
Suddenly a nasty thought,
Deep sigh;
Pleasant thought,
Longing sigh.
The chatters of Hasprays continue like subconscious gossip.
Does mind speak?
Does mind walk?
Sometimes walk speak,
Speak walk.
Who is instigating all this?
Maybe the uranium that makes atom bombs
Shooting star
Allegorical presentation of the dharma
Historical confirmation of the antidisestablishmentarian sophistica-
    tion of the seemingly sane society of the past.

July Fourth
Flash of fireworks—
At the same time,
Lingering thought tells me
My private secretary is really drunk.

Nitpicking
Farfetched—
This rock is problematic:
If it were arranged,
It could complain to the artist;
But since it is not,
No one to sue.
Expectation of the future is too much.
Glory be to somebody's cow dung—
It is too lucid to blame.
There goes everything
Down the drain.

4 July 1975

RMDC, ROUTE 1, LIVERMORE

In the blue sky with no clouds,
The sun of unchanging mind-essence arises;
In the jungle of pine trees swayed by winds,
The birds of chattering thoughts abide;
Among the boulders of immovable dignity,
The insects of subconscious scheming roam;
In the meditation hall many practice dhyana,
Giving birth to realization free of hope and fear.
Through devotion to the only father guru
The place of dharma has been founded,
Abundant with spiritual and temporal powers:
Dead or alive, I have no regrets.

4 July 1975
Rocky Mountain Dharma Center

Translated from the Tibetan (composed earlier the same day).

གེ་སར་ལ་བསྟོད་པ།

གོ་ཁྲབ་གསེར་གྱི་རི་མོས་མཛེས་པ་དང་།

རྟ་མཆོག་ཅང་ཤེས་སྒ་ཡིས་སྒྲས་པ་འདི།

དཔའ་བོ་དམག་དཔོན་ཁྲིད་ལ་གྲགས་པས་འབུལ།

མཐའ་ཡི་དམག་དཔུང་འཇོམས་པའི་ཕྱིར་ལས་མཛོད།

དཔའ་བོ་ཁྲིད་ཀྱི་གཉེན་རྫིང་དེ།

ཚར་སྐྱིན་དགྲས་ཀྱི་གྲོག་ཞགས་འདི།

འཇིགས་པ་ལྟར་ཁྲིད་ཀྱི་འཕྲུ་མ་མདངས་དེ།

བཙོ་ཕྲུའི་ཟླ་བ་ཚེས་པ་འདི།

ཁྲིད་ཀྱི་མཐུ་སྟོབས་ལྷུག་མེད་པ།

རྒྱ་སྟག་གཟན་ལ་ཆགས་པ་འདི།

མདའ་པོའི་དཔུང་གིས་བསྐྱེར་བའི་དབུས།

ཁྲིད་ཉེ་གཡག་གོང་དང་མའདི།

ཁྲིད་ཀྱི་དགྲ་ལ་རང་གྱུར་པ་དེ།

རྒྱུ་སྐྱེགས་རང་ཉིན་པ་འདི།

ཕ་མེས་བརྒྱུད་པ་འཛིན་པའི་ཟུར།

དཔའ་བོ་ཁྲིད་ཀྱིས་སྒྲུལ་སྐྱིབས་མཛོད།

50

TO GESAR OF LING

Armor ornamented with gold designs,
Great horse adorned with sandalwood saddle:
These I offer you, great Warrior General—
Subjugate now the barbarian insurgents.

Your dignity, O Warrior,
Is like lightning in rain clouds.
Your smile, O Warrior,
Is like the full moon.
Your unconquerable power
Is like a tiger springing.
Surrounded by troops,
You are a wild yak.
Becoming your enemy
Is being caught by a crocodile:
O Warrior, protect me,
The ancestral heir.

4 July 1975

*Translated from the Tibetan by the author and David
Rome.*

51

LOVE'S FOOL

Love.
What is love?
What is love.
Love is a fading memory
Love is piercingly present
Love is full of charm
Love is hideously in the way
Explosion of love makes you feel ecstatic
Explosion of love makes you feel suicidal
Love brings goodliness and godliness
Love brings celestial vision
Love creates the unity of heaven and earth
Love tears apart heaven and earth.
Is love sympathy.
Is love gentleness.
Is love possessiveness.
Is love sexuality.
Is love friendship.
Who knows?
Maybe the rock knows
Sitting diligently on earth
Not flinching from cold snowstorms or baking heat.
O rock,
How much I love you:
You are the only loveable one.
Would you let me grow a little flower of love on you?
If you don't mind,
Maybe I could grow a pine tree on you.
If you are so generous,
Maybe I could build a house on you.

If you are fantastically generous,
Maybe I could eat you up,
Or move you to my landscape garden.
It is nice to be friends with a rock.

8 July 1975

52

REPORT FROM LOVELAND

First you like your neighbor,
You have a friendly chat;
Then you are inquisitive,
You begin to compare;
After that you are disturbed
By a lack of harmony;
You hate your neighbor,
Because there are too many mosquitoes in your house.
How silly it is to have a territory in love.
The trouble with you is
That you have forgotten your husband;
The trouble with you is,
You have forgotten your wife.
"Oh this love of datura
It's killing me
But I like it
I would like to keep on with it—
One late night
Drove home
Having been loved
Oh how terrible to be at home
It's chilly
Unfriendly
Feels guilty
But angry
Household articles
Begin to talk to me
My past
My home affairs
My love affair
My wife my husband

Oh shut up!
It's none of your business
You stove
Just get out of my way
You rug
Make yourself invisible
I'm not going to tidy you people up
But
But
But
It's my home
I always want to have a home to come back to
Hell on earth
Hungry ghost
Jealous gods
Human passion
Euphoria of the gods
Stupor of the animals
I thought I was having fun
I'm so innocent
If only I could be with my lover
Nothing would matter
But
The past is haunting me
If I could live in the present
Constant fountain of romance
Nothing would matter
How foolish
How stupid—
Maybe how fantastic."

It all boils down to
Rotten fish beef stew gone bad.
Before we imitate the cuckoos or the pigeons,
We had better think twice
Or thrice.

8 July 1975

53

1018 SPRUCE STREET (and K.A.)

So passionate
That your lips are quivering
So angry
That your blood is boiling
So stupid
That you lost track of your nose
So much so
In this world of so-so
So much
Therefore so little
So little
So great
Just so
The beauty lies in
A rose petal
Just touched by
Melting morning dew
Beauty lies in
Dragonflies
With their double wings
Buzzing neatly
As if they were stationary
Beauty lies in
Majestic shoe
That sits diligently
While the meditators
Torture themselves
In a restless shiver
So right
Norwegian girl

With her occasional professorial look
Dancing with the typewriter
Wife-ing
Just so
With her lukewarm iron
How titillating
(This ticklish world)
Just so.

If you're going to tickle me
Be gentle
Be so precise
So that
I could be amused
But
Wouldn't get hurt
By your clawing
But titillating enough
To stimulate
My system
With your feminine
Healthy shiny
Well-trimmed nail
Just so.

The trees
Grow
Just so
Baby ducks
Learn to float
Just so
Mosquitoes' beaks
Well-made
Just so
Oh you Norwegian girl

Do you know how many warts
On a toad's back?
How many wrinkles
On granddad's forehead?
How many deals
Steve Roth has made?
Nothing to worry
Everything is
Just so
Doesn't quite hurt
But sometimes
Painfully ticklish.

28 July 1975

1135 10TH STREET (and G.M.)

How nice it is to meet an old friend,
How refreshing to see an old friend;
Meeting an old friend is much better than discovering new ones—
Passing an old stone
On the winding mountain road,
Passing an old oak tree
In the English country garden,
Passing a derelict castle
On the French hillside,
Passing an old ant
On the sidewalk—
Glory be to Giovannina!
Maybe all this is a castle in the air,
Maybe this is my conceptualized preconceived subconscious
	imaginary expectation,
Maybe this is just a simple blade of grass.
It is all very touching.
Maybe it is just glue,
Glorified glue
That glues heaven and earth together,
Glue that seals great cracks in the Tower of London.
However,
There is something nice about Giovannina:
When she smiles,
She cheers up the depressed pollution;
When she talks,
She proclaims the wisdom of precision.
She is somewhat small,
But dynamite.
She seems to know who she is.

She could create thunderstorm;
She could produce gentle rain.
She could get you good property;
She brings down the castle in the air.
She is somehow in my opinion well-manufactured.
Fresh air of the Alps—
I think she is fresh air,
Which turns into a well-cared-for garden
Free from lawn mowers and insecticides.

30 July 1975

1111 PEARL STREET (and D.S.)

Our anxiety,
Our case history,
Our problems with the world—
We tried so hard to accomplish,
We tried very hard.
But now we are a sitting rock in the midst of rain;
We are the broom in the closet;
We are just leaves rejected by an autumn tree.
Sometimes we think highly of ourselves—
Thundering typhoons!
Glory be to Captain Haddock,
Punished for not being crazy enough,
Sent to jail for being crazy.
Does a pitchfork have a blade?
Do the handcuffs have emotions?
Persecuted by your own guilt,
Uplifted by your chauvinism—
The whole thing is a bag full of razorblades and pebbles.

August 1975

78 FIFTH AVENUE

It was a desolate space you provided today;
It was hearty, but sadly WASP.
The subtle air of power is devastating
In the midst of the Black Velvet advertisement.
It is a rewarding experience that you are not on a billboard,
But a breathing human being
Who produce a star on your nose as you sweat.
Our meeting was like a lady rider having a chat with a horse in its
      stall
With the atmosphere of potent dung, refreshing hay,
While the neighboring horse, clad in a tartan blanket, looked on.
This desolate concrete cemetery that you claim is your birthplace—
I feel you deserve more than this:
Rebars and concrete facades,
Eternally farting cars spreading pollution,
Yellow cabs producing their own aggression for the sake of money
      and legality—
You should be sitting on rocks
Where the heathers grow, daisies take their delight, clovers roam
      around and pine trees drop their needles of hints.
You deserve a better world than what you have.
I would like to take you for a ride in my world,
My heroic world:
We ride in a chariot adorned with the sun, the moon and the four
      elements;
We take a great leap as we ride;
We are not timid people;
We are not trapped in our beauty or profession.
Oh you—

Your corrupted purity is still immaculate from a layman's point of
  view.
However, I am not a layman:
I am a lover.
Let us chew together a blade of chive—
You could take me out for dinner next.
Heaven forbid!
Gosh! as they say.
Suddenly I miss you.
Do you miss me?
You miss
I miss
You miss
I miss
You miss
I miss
Should you miss me?
Should I miss you?
It's all a mutual game.
If you miss me, maintain your is-ness.
When I see you next, I want to see you exactly the same as I saw you
  now.
But that is too foolish—
Let us come to an agreement:
If I miss you, you will be slightly different;
If you miss me, I will be slightly different.
Let us meet each other in our growth and aging.
In any case, let us build the Empire State Building on top of the
  Continental Divide.

22 March 1976
New York City

Shar (*East*)

57

THE ALDEN (and Thomas Frederick)

I hand you my power;
If I grow you grow.
Your childishness is the ground where you can take part in the
    power.
Your inquisitiveness is magnificent.
There is need for a further growing tie with heaven and earth.
I have given you the space,
The very blue sky;
The clouds and the suns and the moons are yours.
But you are confused,
You like more toys:
Should they be made of gold, or plastic?
Should they come from New Jersey, or from the collections of the
    British court?
Could you use your responsibility as a golden joke, or a vajra
    scepter?
It is very heavy,
But I think you can hold it.
Canoeing is not for you,
Maybe parachuting.
Embroidering is not for you,
Maybe executing.
You, my son,
Take your Swiss Army knife—
Make a samurai sword out of it.

22 March 1976

58

COMMENTARY ON
"THE ALDEN (and Thomas Frederick)"

I hand you my power:
> When I gave you an inch, that symbolized a mile;
> I am glad you accept me and my mileage.

If I grow you grow:
> If my kingdom grows, you will be hassled by it;
> You will be forced to grow.

Your childishness is the ground where you can take part in the power:
> Your innocence and willingness are the only working basis
>   we have;
> Therefore, I hope you will be corrupted and cynical,
>   which is good.

Your inquisitiveness is magnificent:
> You have not been embarrassed by a wooden nickel,
> But you are so inquisitive about how I manage my world;
> I am proud that I can push you into the world of elegance.

There is need for a further growing tie with heaven and earth:
> Your smelly socks are due to having dandruff in your hair;
> Please don't regard this as problematic:
> We should have head and feet together.

I have given you the space:
> Since there is no choice—
> Space is not mine but yours too;
> But in my case, I pretended that I owned it,
> And gave it to you as my hearty gift.

The very blue sky:
> In the world of dharmadhatu everything is blue;
> You I felt as the inheritor of our lineages.

The clouds and the suns and the moons are yours:
> The organization of clouds, suns of your insight and
>   moons of challenge:
> To work among these three;
> However, this is not passing the buck;
> I regard this as passing the family heirloom—
> If I may say so, you should be proud of it.

But you are confused:
> Too many gifts and complimentary remarks make you like a
>   cross-eyed owl, or frog, for that matter;
> But don't take it too seriously—
> The confusion is powerfully yours.

You like more toys:
> Tinkle tinkle toy world is glorious but hard-core
>   toy world is depressing—
> They are all made out of plastic anyway;
> Don't you think there's something unpleasant about that?

Should they be made of gold, or plastic?
> Should they be?
> Even though they may be made out of gold, it is plastic—
> You have better taste than that, Ösel.

Should they come from New Jersey, or from the collections of the British court?
> I would prefer they come from the British court,
> But then you should be involved in a different court;
> Maybe New Jersey is too familiar to you;
> Don't be so crazy about cosmopolitanness—
> They have their own rotten history.

*Could you use your responsibility as a golden joke, or a vajra
     scepter?*
          This is a one-sided question: obviously the vajra scepter;
          The golden joke of the other cosmopolitan trips is pretty funky,
          I hope you know that.

It is very heavy:
          It is demanding;
          It does not provide you with a smile, but you have to provide it
               with your own smile—
          But do we know what "it" is?

But I think you can hold it:
          Don't have domestic orgasm but but but hold it—
          Let us have cosmic orgasm with a giant splash:
          Don't you think that's a good idea with a vajra scepter in your
               hand?

Canoeing is not for you:
          You should swim, you should do equitation, you should do
               archery;
          But diving together with hippy-dippy canoeing-trippy
          is outdated for you,
          Don't you think so?

Maybe parachuting:
          Ah! There's something for you, you could do this:
          Parachuting, literally or metaphorically;
          I know you like the drop and I know you like the float—
          Maybe we could do them together at some point.

Embroidering is not for you:
          Little stitches are very much of low vision.

Maybe executing:
          You would be a great executor;
          You are a great officer in executive committee:
          I'm sure that is a good job for you—
          You have done it already in any case.

You, my son:
>   Did you know your father was I?
>   But in any case, who can transcend the affection beyond sonship
>   but you?

Take your Swiss Army knife:
>   Made in Switzerland, all sorts of possibilities:
>   Goodly made, efficient, well-thought-out, everything you could
>   think of,
>   My gift to you,
>   Which says T.G.S. on the handle as well.

Make a samurai sword out of it:
>   Be a good swordsman.

20 August 1976
Boulder, Colorado

On the occasion of the empowerment of the Vajra Regent Ösel Tendzin.

AURORA 7 (#2)

Sun is dead,
Moon is born;
Moon is dead,
Sun is born.
Who said that?
Which is true.
Sun-moon are alive,
Sun-moon are dead;
They both shine on their own schedules.
Chögyam is alive;
No hope for the death of Chögyam—
Taking care of Chögyie
With hot warm towels
Breakfast in bed
Chamber pots in their proper places
Serving Chögyie as the precious jewel who may not stay with us—
All take part in the platitude of serving Chögyie as a dying person!
Oh! What's become of Chögyie?
He drinks too much,
He's bound to die soon—
Taking care of Chögyie is no longer would-be mother's pleasure?
Thriving strongly,
Existing powerfully,
Eternally growing,
Stainless steel veins:
Chögyie is a crystal ball with stainless steel veins,
With diamond heart.
Even the most accomplished samurais' swords can't cut Chögyie's
     veins,
Because his veins are vajra metal,

The blood is liquid ruby.
The indestructibility of Chögyie is settled—
For foes very frightening:
Downfall of him never occurs;
For friends rejoicing:
Chögyie is made out of vajra nature.
Such good Chögyie makes people shed their tears;
Such good Chögyie makes people tremble before his vajra dignity.
Chögyie is going to be pain and pleasure for all of you,
Whether you hate or love him.
Chögyie's indestructibility could be venom as well as longevity-nectar.
Here comes Chögyie,
Chögyie's for all,
Take Chögyie as yours—
Chögyam says: Lots of love!
I'm yours!

8 April 1976

1111 PEARL STREET
OFF BEAT

In the clear atmosphere,
A dot occurred.
Passion tinged that dot vermilion red,
Shaded with depression pink.
How beautiful to be in the realm of nonexistence:
When you dissolve, the dot dissolves;
When you open up, clear space opens.
Let us dissolve in the realm of passion,
Which is feared by the theologians and lawmakers.
Pluck, pluck, pluck, pluck the wild flower.
It is not so much of orgasm,
But it is a simple gesture,
To realize fresh mountain air that includes the innocence of a wild
    flower.
Come, come, D.I.R., you could join us.
The freshness is not a threat, not a burden;
It is a most affectionate gesture—
That a city could dissolve in love of the wildness of country flowers.
No duty, no sacrifice, no trap;
The world is full of trustworthy openness.
Let us celebrate in the cool joy
The turquoise blue
Morning dew
Sunny laughter
Humid home:
Images of love are so good and brilliant.

June 1976

AURORA 7 (and Nyingje Sheltri)

When a cold knife is planted in your heart,
What do you say to it?
When you have swallowed a cold stone,
What do you say to it?
When you have swallowed a cold icicle,
When you feel love hurts,
What do you say to it?
This kind of hurt, is it pleasurable?
Pain pleasure
Pleasure pain
Cold hurt
Hurt cold
Hurt hot
Hot hurt—
Wish I had never experienced blue sky or green grass,
Beautiful lover (would-be).
Would such hurt, gut hurt, throat hurt, brain hurt, lung hurt, such
    hurt hurt,
Bring about cosmic love affair one of these days?
Maybe the bleeding part should be served as dessert,
With occasional bubble, occasional odor
And occasional music played with it.
Such hurt love is so love love hurt.
Maybe frogs have never experienced this;
The Pekingese, the poodles are lucky
That nobody killed themselves being lovesick.

You hurt
You tingle me
You tingle hurt

Hurt tingle
Tingle hurty
Hurt tingly
Pain
Lust
Love
Passion
Red
Ruby
Blood
Ruby lust
Lust cold
Cold ruby
Frozen rose
Rose frozen
Lust passion
Cold hate
Hate ruby
Passion lust cold hate ruby
Hot ruby lust
Flute hot
Lust flute
Cold icicle
Hot ruby lust passion cold flute
Pure
Pure ruby
Pure hot cold ruby
Lust passion pure cold ruby
Cheat
Hot cheat
Cheat convert
Hot passion cheat
Cheat blood
Cheating blood
Passion ruby flute

Cold hot flute
Play
Hot play
Cheat play
Cheat play hot passion ruby
Drum
Thunder
Thunder drum
Drum thunder
Hot drum hot cheat
Hot cheat ruby drum
Drum drum drum
Cheat drum ruby
Cheat hot passion
Ruby hot piss
Flute
The flute
Throbbing flute
Throbbing heart
Cheat throbbing heart
Hot cheat throbbing passion flute
Throbbing sex
Passion ruby
Deaf
Mute
Mute passion
Deaf passion
Throbbing deaf mute passion in cold ruby liquid.

3 August 1976

PAN-AMERICAN DHARMADHATU III

Thick oak tree trunk
Is hard to break with two hands.
Thick oak ego
Skandha tree trunk
Is easier to break by the two hands of the vajra master.
Farmingdale
Thistledale
Heatherdale
Lovely sites beautiful to look at:
That is Dharmadhatu.
Some Dharmadhatus are tall and skinny,
Colored with luscious leaves;
Some Dharmadhatus are fat and stocky,
Weighted with delicious fruit;
Some Dharmadhatus are thorny and tough,
Dotted with bright berries;
Some Dharmadhatus are bending,
Swayed by wind;
Some Dharmadhatus are upright,
Growing in the midst of a giant forest.
Oh such Dharmadhatu jungle—
It is beautiful.
Wandering in the Dharmadhatu forest
You meet meek chipmunks
Humorous porcupines
Delicate magpies
Sneaky squirrels
Powerful tigers
Exotic jackals
Manipulative ants

Doing their own little duties right and left.
It is quite an experience to be in the midst of Dharmadhatu jungle.
Glory be to the Forestry Department of Vajradhatu,
That such jungle has been taken care of and appreciated.
However, dry twigs and wounded branches need to be pruned,
So that we could nurse the cosmic universal pan-American
     Dharmadhatu jungle.
It is nice to be a jungle man,
Tree warrior.
I send my love to the invincible perpetuating jungle of Dharmadhatus.

4 October 1976
Land O' Lakes, Wisconsin

TIBETAN LYRICS

Like a hunting dog, my friend,
You are always hungry, hoping for me.
The weather is good today:
Vanish to the distant jungle.

Yesterday I did not offer you tea,
Today I ask you not to be angry;
Tomorrow, if the weather is good,
Together we will go to battle.

This black stallion of mine:
If you ride it to the plain, it is like the shadow of a bird;
If you ride it to the mountain, it is like a flame;
If you ride it to the water, it is like a fish;
If you ride it to the sky, it is like a white cloud.
When ornamented with a saddle, it is like a king
        setting out to battle.
This is an excellent great horse—
Out of delight and respect, I offer it to you.

1976

ASLEEP AND AWAKE

While the grass was falling asleep
Waiting for the snowflakes,
Timid world has been reshaped into warrior world:
My accomplishment is achieved.
Abundance of sympathy, devotion, kindness, politeness—
All amount to asleep and awake.
When dying culture is reintroduced,
It becomes genuinely powerful.

11 February 1977

GREAT EASTERN DAUGHTERLET

When I discovered her,
She was one,
And when I searched for her,
She was ten;
When I sent for her,
She was fifteen;
When I invited her,
She was nineteen;
When I discovered her unicorn's horn,
She was twenty-five;
When I taught her the English language,
She was fifty;
When I taught her how to walk,
She was seventy;
When I told her that she is the daughter of Shambhala,
She was one hundred and two;
So much for her age.
She still remains nineteen years old—
Princess who possesses the delightful white face of the highland
    moose.

3 June 1977
Ingonish, Nova Scotia

WHYCOCOMAGH?

Sometimes there are trees;
Sometimes there are rocks;
However, occasionally there are lakes;
Always, to be sure, there are houses;
To be sure certain there are views of a certain gentleman being
    crucified.
Nevertheless, the deep-fried food is very decent,
So good that one almost forgets bourgeois cuisine.

The coastal sky seems to frown at us
With its benevolent threat;
We receive plentiful rain.
In green valley pastures brown cows graze.
Tibetan-tea-like rough rivers carry the highland soil.
Occasional mist and fog bring wondrous possibilities.
Naive hitchhikers laugh and scrutinize our convoy.
The highlands are beautiful, free from pollution,
The lowlands regular, telling the whole truth:
There is nothing to hide.
Harmonious province hangs together,
But for occasional economic panic.
Men of Shambhala would feel comfortable and confident in the
    province of no big deal,
Flying the banner of St. Andrew adorned with the lion of Scotland,
    red and yellow.
We find it beyond conflict to fly the banner of the Great Eastern Sun.

It is curious to see their flags strung on yellow cords;
Nice to watch the children cycling in the ditch;
Nice to discover all the waiters serving on their first day;
Nice to see that nobody is apologetic;
Good to see alders taking root after the forest fire of pines.

June 1977
New Glasgow, Nova Scotia

LION'S ROAR

Genuine people bring genuine intellect,
Genuine mind brings genuine discipline,
Genuine teacher and student bring true wisdom;
Naropa the great siddha brought the spotless discipline of the Prac-
    tice Lineage.
Theory is empty head without brains,
Chatting logicians are the parrot flock,
Clever psychologists swallow their own tongues,
Chic artists manufacture garbage collages—
At this illustrious Institute we are free from confusion.
Let us celebrate in the name of sanity,
Let us proclaim the true discipline,
Let us rejoice:
The eternally rising sun is everpresent.
In the name of the lineage, I rejoice.

17 August 1977

Composed for the first graduation ceremony of Naropa Institute.

68

TIMELY RAIN

In the jungles of flaming ego,
May there be cool iceberg of bodhicitta.

On the racetrack of bureaucracy,
May there be the walk of the elephant.

May the sumptuous castle of arrogance
Be destroyed by vajra confidence.

In the garden of gentle sanity,
May you be bombarded by coconuts of wakefulness.

20 October 1977

PAN-DHARMADOLLAR

Looking for cheaper restaurants,
Paying for expensive ties,
Are dualistic as much as Mohammed and the mountain.
Would the mountain come to Mohammed
Or Mohammed go to the mountain?
Sadat and Begin made a pact,
But who is going to achieve peace?
Vision and dollar are in conflict:
When there are lots of dollars,
There is no vision;
When there are no dollars,
There is lots of vision.
Clearly stranded,
Goodly rich,
Goodly poor,
Can't afford to pay for one's own tuxedo,
Can pay for one's luxury in the realm of buddhadharma,
Elegant waltz participation,
Contradiction after contradiction.
Why is a parrot green,
Speaking human language?
Why is the monkey ambidextrous,
Mocking humans?
Why do Americans mock the vajra kingdom?
They don't mean to,
They are merely being casual because they have no money,
Or they have too much money;
Therefore, they can come up with cheap proposals.
Will this go down in our history?
No.

The Noh play says:
Worshipping every deity is trusting in ancestral heritage.

For the cosmopolitan communication of dharma,
Let us have lots of ratna.
For the hermit who is in the cave in order to perpetuate the practice,
Let us have lots of ratna.
For the scholars who are translating buddhadharma into Americanism,
Let us have lots of ratna.
For the householder yogis who could practice tantra with indestructi-
    ble conviction,
Let us have lots of ratna.
For the freelancers who might give up their ego trips,
To accommodate and lure them into the dharma world,
Let us have lots of ratna.
For the young maidens who fall in love with the dharmic man,
To create a truly genuine dharmic world,
Let us have lots of ratna.
For the warriors who fight for the sake of Shambhala kingdom,
Who never leave their prajna swords behind,
Let us have lots of ratna.
For the administrator who never breathes for his own sake,
But is purely concerned about the facts and figures and morality of
    our organization of the vajra mandala,
Let us have lots of ratna.
For the vajra master who couldn't exist without the vajra world,
    dedicating his life and yet receiving longevity nectar from others,
Let us have lots of ratna.
Money peeps,
Money tweaks,
However, money has never roared.
Lion's roar could be money.
Pay!
Due!
Accelerate!

Save!
Complain!
Bargain!
Let us save money by spending,
Let us spend by saving:
Sane money is free from dualistic territory.
For the Great Eastern Sun, frigid money is no good.
Computerized this and that is a kid playing cowboys and Indians:
Let us relax and be taut in our money world.
May there be Sukhavati of dollars.
May there be Shambhala kingdom with lots of wealth—
But wealth comes from waltz,
Waltz comes from dignity,
Dignity comes from consideration,
Consideration comes from being sane.
Let us spend,
Let us save:
The Great Eastern Sun saves and radiates.
Good for you—
Jolly good show to everyone—
Let us be genuine.

3 December 1977

MEETINGS WITH REMARKABLE PEOPLE

Banana aluminium,
Wretched secondhand pressure cooker,
Crucifixions made out of plastic,
Jumbo jet,
Iron grid that is fit for cooking but not for eating, with a permanent
    garlic stain,
Rooster with its feathers and flashy crest and waddles of elegant pink
    flashy brocade—
Sometimes we wonder whether we should be one of those,
Or else should completely fake the whole thing.
The gentleman with slim mustache and note pad under his arm
Told us that we shouldn't fake anything,
Otherwise we are going to run into trouble with BDS as well as IRS.
The gentleman with belly button, weighing 300 pounds,
Told us that if we're going to fake anything,
We had better cut our aortas first.
A lady too told us the same thing;
She was wearing a tigerskin skirt,
She had a giant smile but one tooth,
She had turquoise hair but elegant gaze
From her single eye,
She was drooping,
She seemed to be wearing some kind of lipstick and powder make-up,
Her earlobes were big,
She was wearing giant gold earrings—
She told us they were 24 carat
And she complained that they were sometimes too heavy on her
    head;
She also told us that her hair was unmanageable,
That her neck muscles have too much blood power;

However, she stood there telling us all those things.
She brought along a companion of hers,
A lovely maiden wearing a necklace of pearl,
Smiling, with a light complexion,
Riding on a white lion.
Then she brought a third friend who was very peculiar:
One wonders whether he was man or woman, human or animal;
He had a most gaping mouth opening at his stomach,
With somewhat polite gaze;
He possessed nine heads,
All of them expressing certain expressions
And wearing conch-shell rings in their earlobes;
When you look at him, his faces have the same expressions,
But with seeming distortion in every face of delight.
Can you imagine seeing such people and receiving and talking to
     them?
Ordinarily, if you told such stories to anybody, they would think
     you were a nut case;
But, in this case, I have to insist that I am not a nut case:
I witnessed these extraordinary three friends in the flesh.
Surprisingly, they all spoke English;
They had no problem in communicating in the midst of American
     surroundings.
I am perfectly certain that they are capable of turning off the light or
     turning on the television.
What do you say about this whole thing?
Don't you think meeting such sweet friends is worthwhile and
     rewarding?
Moreover, they promise me that they will protect me all along.
Don't you think they are sweet?
And I believe them, that they can protect me.
I would say meeting them is meeting with remarkable men and
     women:
Let us believe that such things do exist.

8 December 1977

INTERNATIONAL AFFAIRS
THE COSMIC JOKE OF 1977

In this godforsaken place so-called planet Earth,
Rainstorms thundershowers snowfreeze floods and typhoons constantly occur.
Somewhere there is good harvest, somewhere there is famine,
Shortage of something-or-other,
Aberfan chaos,
Liverpool dock strike,
Sheffield problem with the stainless steel workers.
Jesuits in China were kicked out by the Communists.
Catholics do hard work in Thailand, but the Buddhist school system makes it ineffective.
Sri Lanka is having a paranoia with the Sacred Heart people.
Mr. Park experiences slap on the face from trying to buy the U.S. senators.
Indira Gandhi is fading in Desai's pollution with bhajans of Gandhi supplication.
Sadat is trying to trick the world but stepping on the dog-shit of Arab manure.
Madame Mao with her coyote true-believing hunting expedition has been caught by the suburban Hua.
Dung Hsiao Peng is resurrected like the Christ and planning capitalized Communism.
Moscow proclaims its steady Kremlin victory, which was won sixty years ago.
Brezhnev half-dead thinking that he is a good huntsman and the greatest general in the world,
Choking with Stalinist nostalgia,
Nixon dead corpse has made American statesman into Carter embarrassment;

Maybe George Washington did lie occasionally.

Human rights program is not all that religious, since nobody in the world believes in true-believing any more.

Jimmy cardigan approach does not work in conflict with Congress's suit and tie.

Trudeau trumpet did not provide fanfare for the Quebecois because one note was missing—

The French homemade folksong.

Hong Kong cannot be repossessed because the Chinese fear unity between U.S. and U.K.

Japan cannot make Australasia connections because they felt a bad slap after the Second World War;

Sony and Mitsubishi might save their own lives, but they are doubtfully courageous.

German boldness is hooha, yet good living in the Deutschland provides a reason to be against the North Sea oil of the U.K.

France like a drunken sheep perpetually propagates François;

Giscard posing with his daughter for a campaign portrait worked, but dining with citizens seemed to end quite abruptly.

MIG Mirage Phantom and the vertical take-off of the English do not work in the sale of arms because Arabs have lopsided the purchase.

Maybe King Hussein is the shrewdest customer for all these things;

But since Hussein is questionably sane or not, no doubt the Russians will do double takes on all this.

Burma's Ne Win feels that he is able to contain the Buddhists while courting socialism by being polite to the Chinese.

The Cambodian Prince is whispering about his royal position in the country, while his activities are proscribed by the party of the delirious generals and the circumcised party members.

Madame Mao had a slight problem, to say the least, when she tried to ban classical Chinese opera.

Rhodesians try to compensate by being good and bad at the same time, with seeming kind hatred to their natives.

South Africa is cooped up with a big gun and no one to shoot
    except the wall where the gun is;

Black majority means that soul food might be tastier than roast beef
    and Yorkshire pudding.

Britain experiences cosmic shock with the problem of existence and
    nonexistence—

The only saving grace is Her Majesty the Queen in marketing her
    underpants,

Which might work for a while, but still is questionable:

Will Charles be referred to as Chuck?

Kingdom of Spain:

Carlos has his own tortilla—to make his mind up about jumping to
    the conclusion of the Communists;

It is uncertain whether he is the tortilla or the leftists are his tortilla—

Being too good does not help;

Generalissimo has no doubt appeared to Carlos many times in vision
    after his death.

Mongolians in Ulan Bator have felt that as long as they kept with the
    Russians they were safe,

But their nerve center has begun to leak to the Chinese People's
    Republic;

It would be much better for them to milk horses as they have done:

Good cheese might come out of that.

And what about the United Nations?

We begin to feel the United Nations is not even a great apple strudel.

The United Nations is shortcake;

It is well-cooked seafood without wasabi.

The United Nations is a well-brewed nonexistent alcohol that no-
    body will drink.

However, union of nations might provide some hope and fear so
    that we could actually respect it as more than a buffer,

As Baha'ullah would say.

The United Nations seems to be a garbage chute;

The United Nations is a dilettante true-believer in the world's unity;

The United Nations is a giant building in New York City, but nobody knows what's happening inside;

On the whole we could say the United Nations is pampas grass that grows around a Japanese garden.

There is no reason to criticize, because the United Nations doesn't provoke any bravery;

The United Nations is a gentleman's underpants: nobody dares to criticize or cultivate;

The United Nations is good theory but not good practice;

The United Nations provides good school, but naughty children can throw ink blops at the teacher while having no basic unity.

Jimmy Carter gave a splendid talk at the United Nations;

Khrushchev pounded his shoe on the desk;

Idi Amin vomited his rhetoric at the General Assembly;

The Pope sanctified the United Nations, telling them that peace and godliness are the only way;

The Dalai Lama was rejected by the United Nations.

Flying the colors of all the countries, the United Nations looks heroic and beautiful,

But its own blue and white feels grey and beige.

Receiving the complaints of all countries, the United Nations becomes a polite wasteland.

Since the absence of U Thant the United Nations is a fish-and-chip shop where all nations are expected to add sugar instead of vinegar.

In this case, the world is ending—

What shall we do about it?

Let us bring the Great Eastern Sun, with or without the United Nations.

Let us have champagne breakfasts celebrating the rising sun.

Hail to the Union of Nations!

Hail to the Union of Nations!

Hail to the Union of Nations!

December 1977
Charlemont, Massachusetts

129

72

One sound

One sound
Thousand ripples—
Taizan jumps in the sand.

December 1977

73

DIXVILLE NOTCH

PURRINGTON HOUSE (and C.F.)

A glowing worm is said to be brilliant,
But the brilliant sun is more convincing;
Sweet smile seems to be the best,
But genuine affection is more convincing.
When I was riding with you
On that winding road of our mutual snow mountain,
You said, "Oops!"
I said, "What?"
Nonetheless we are both fascinated and intrigued by our mutual trip,
Fueled by immense passion and a glowing sense of humor.
We might find snowdrops somewhere:
You said you didn't like the melting snow,
You said you liked the fresh snow—
I was intrigued by the way your constructive mind worked.
While gazing at an icicle,
At first a little one on its way, melting,
You then discovered that little one becoming bigger:
Such rediscovery of the phenomenal world and appreciation of detail—
Indra and Brahma and Avalokiteshvara
Would have found this appreciation so sweet and glowing.

When we met,
You were merely there;
When we talked,
You were tongue-tied.
And again when we met,
You were more than there;
When we talked,
You were very articulate.

Our mutual guess became like the dance of the dragonfly:
You guessed,
I guessed;
Did anybody guess?
Did anyone guess?
Sometimes one wonders whether we should give away this mutual
    secret to anybody.

Spring gives way to summer
And summer gives way to autumn;
Autumn gives way to winter:
Then we are back to square one,
Watching icicles again.

When you are attacked by this and that,
You should hold the needle of nowness
Threaded with our mutual passion.
When you are hungry and fearful of the small big world,
You should look at the Great Eastern Sun
With the eye of our mutual passion.
When you are lonely,
You should beat the drum of sanity
With the stick of our mutual passion.
When you feel awkward,
You should drink the sake of confidence
With the lips of our mutual passion.
When you feel you are nobody,
You should hold the falcon of great humor
With the hand of our mutual passion.
When you feel spoiled,
You should fly the banner of genuineness
With the wind of our mutual passion.

You should have no problem in propagating our mutual passion—
As long as, or as short as,

A journey's been made
In the name of the biggest or the smallest,
Which transcends eruption of stomach.
Peacock magpie wolf
Rattlesnakes equipped with antennae
Jackal polar bear shaggy dog
Taj Mahal
Good wasabi
Chicken feet
Rothman's Special—
All of these, wicked and workable, are our world.
Including all those there is no problem,
Whether the so-called phenomenal world is sweet or sour, painful or
     pleasurable.
We should make sure that we do not put them in the oven
And make a convenient loaf of bread of them.
Let us not regard the world as one,
Or, for that matter, let us not regard the world as multiple.
As long as we dance and sing, sweep the floor, wash the dirty dishes
And celebrate in the name of satin silk diamond ruby emerald and
     pearls,
Fresh water clinking with ice,
We are producing rich cold powerful ideal world,
With a touch of warmness:
Let us project to this universe our mutual passion.

If I may go further:
We are not deaf, not dumb,
We are not mute.
We are the world's best possible goodness—
Outspoken, exaggerated, understated fanfare,
With the goodness of goodness.
The wicked will tremble and the good will celebrate:
Impossibility is accomplished in the realm of possibility—
Fathomless space being measured,

Depth of passion being explored.
Let us eat snail adorned with fortune cookies;
Let us drink amrita fizzed with our mutual humor.
Let us ride the horse of delightful disestablished world,
Saddled with our mutual passion.

Did you know the sun rises in the East?
Don't believe those who tell you that the sun rises in the West.
Shall we have our mutual celebration?
One who fights is eternally poor;
One who shares is victorious:
Let us celebrate in our mutual passion.

21 March 1978

AFTERTHOUGHT

Such a precious human body,
Difficult to rediscover;
Such precious pain,
Not difficult to discover;
Such an old story
Is by now a familiar joke.
You and I know the facts and the case history;
We have a mutual understanding of each other
Which has never been sold or bought by anyone.
Our mutual understanding keeps the thread of sanity.
Sometimes the thread is electrified,
Sometimes it is smeared with honey and butter;
Nevertheless, we have no regrets.
Since I am here,
Seemingly you are here too.
Let us practice!
Sitting is a jewel that ornaments our precious life.

21 March 1978

DON'T CONFUSE THIS FOR TRICK-OR-TREAT

Those who sit
Shouldn't be cowards,
Those who sit
Shouldn't be tricky,
Those who sit
Shouldn't be resourceful,
Those who sit
Should be basic people
Who sit—
But no tricks of
Tricky
Fuzzy
Jumpy
Creepy
Thinking
Funny:
Sitters in the buddhadharma world
Should be decent.

I met a sitter who said
She could build the Buddhist version of Disneyland—
If we would permit her not to sit for at least forty-five minutes.

I met a sitter who said,
"I could ape like a monkey, growl like a tiger;
I could huff and puff and get lots of money for Vajradhatu—
If you would permit me not to sit for at least forty-five minutes."

I met a sitter who shrieked like a loon,
Who said,

"I don't like what's going on. I never did.
Either I have room to fix things up or I'll quit.
In any case, *I* want to be acknowledged—
If you would permit me not to sit for at least forty-five minutes."

I met a sitter who is a foogy-doogy owl,
Who said,
"Come to think of it,
I don't like the administration because they make me sit.
On the whole, I prefer not to be manipulated by the establishment.
I feel fooled and conned, wretched and abused.
I prefer not to see the daylight—
If only you would permit me not to sit for at least forty-five
    minutes."

I met a sitter who has developed a snout like a jackal,
Who said,
"I would like to collect the crumbs;
I would like to explore them,
So that I could feel whether the Vajrayana makes sense.
These crumbs of Hinayana and Mahayana are worthwhile.
I prefer to regurgitate, and I would be delighted to eat up my own
    vomit,
And quite possibly I could take it home in lunch-packs
And have a good holiday—
If only you would permit me not to sit for at least forty-five
    minutes."

I met a sitter who is a prairie dog,
Who said,
"This madhyamika logic and Buddhist reasoning is like eating ants
    as opposed to collecting nuts.
I don't like theory anyway;
I would like to have nutshells—
If only you would permit me not to sit for at least forty-five
    minutes."

137

I met a sitter who is an oily cat,
Who said,
"This Vajra Politics is for the stupid seagulls.
I would prefer to meow rather than fly and caw.
I feel threatened by being fed.
I prefer to do my own hunting:
You can swallow a few poisons here and there in hunting—
If only you would permit me not to sit for at least forty-five
    minutes."

Many people scheme,
Trying to occupy,
Trying to use logical mind.
But when you sit,
These schemes begin to turn into cow's dung,
Which might have good manure possibilities.
Other than that,
We find nobody has developed the lucky strike.
We have to keep on sitting,
All the time.
Sit all the time.
Day time.
Night time.
Early.
Late.
In the midst of your dream.
Who could care less that you're sitting so much?
Somebody might be thankful that you're sitting so much.
Sunrise.
Sunset.
Good days.
Bad days.
Making a mockery of your self-indulgence and ingenuity.
Good manipulation
Good reestablishment

Of your missing the point in the midst of your own yawn.
Fundamentally there are no sympathizers who will accept your lucky
    wormstrike:
Lucky cozychickengooddumplinghoneylakeincrediblygoodmassage-
    goodbreakgoodbreathingspaceallareyourtricksanyway.
Nobody gets anybody.
Good wasabi.

We pre-smart you before you outsmart us.
Everybody knows what you're trying to get at.
All the tricks are predictably silly.
So let us celebrate in our silly tricks—
Hallelujah!
Corny tricks and trips are bad noodles.
Try better next time,
If you can at all.

22 March 1978
Vajradhatu Seminary
Dixville Notch, New Hampshire

ETERNAL GUEST

In the jungle of passion,
The warrior of the tiger roams;
In the flame of aggression,
The diamond vajra sparks;
In the ocean of ignorance,
The iceberg of cold awake rumbles.
Bounded by love
Swallows still try to measure the sky;
Nursed with the nectar of amrita,
Still we look for a nanny goat's nipples—
Such as we are:
But we do not give up.

We should not give up:
We are the children of the vajra world.
We should sing the anthem of lion's roar;
We should cry the shriek of fearlessness.
Come and join us!
Let us be wakeful for our own sake;
Let us be decent for others' sake.
My love to you.

6 April 1978

SWALLOWING THE SUN AND MOON
WITHOUT LEAVING THE WORLD IN DARKNESS
GOOD LADY OF WISDOM

Crooks have their way of handling their world;
Honest ones will stitch and sew timidly.
Crooks have a way to proclaim their victory;
But the honest stumble, bump and stutter.
Crooks have their way to dress in nouveau-riche fashion;
But the honest wash, clean and press.
Crooks have their way to kick, knock, run;
The honest will take a taxicab.
The crooks will assume, expect and consume;
The honest will speak softly with timid smiles.
The crooks are usually dirty, oiled with their own sweat;
The honest are clean, well-groomed—at least free of dandruff.
We have a lot of reference points here—
However, I would suggest you swallow the sun and moon simulta-
    neously.
That does not mean you are a crook,
But an honest man not wasting time.

Since we met, I have been trying to make you an honest person.
You had your little ways;
Your being honest is wicked.
Sometimes I wonder who taught you that:
Maybe your Canadian honest crooks,
Or your crooked honest Canadians.
However, someone talked you into being a timid person.
Some quarters of theism would say:
If you are a person of proclamation in early life, it is bad;
You should not take anything, even if it is given to you;

You should say thank you for everything, even if it is yours;
You should learn to say no thank you if things are not yours;
You are supposed to watch your P's and Q's if things are uncertain.
In short, you should not hurt a flea;
If a flea is your neighbor, turn the other cheek.
Nevertheless, if there is a big disagreement,
You should not hesitate to cut his throat
And disbelievers in Christendom are animals—
You might as well make good Yorkshire pudding out of them.

However, when your shoe walks without you
And your hat floats without you,
You wonder who's in them.
I think you should be startled,
You have a perfect right to be startled.
We're not joking, are we?
Of course not.

Buddha died in bed;
Christ died on the cross;
However, you might die in bed on a cross.
We shouldn't be too concerned with little details like that.
Let's turn the whiskers of cat,
Polish the nails of poodle.
Let's not tiptoe, anyhow.
Take a big chunk out of my life;
Make a good cake out of it.
Let us roll in a kingsize snowbed,
Let us sniff Mitsuko,
Let us pluck hair off the tiger's back,
Let us eat sausage of Brahman bull,
Let us catch the sun with a net,
Let us catch the moon with bait,
Let us not tiptoe.
Since your world is mine,

There is no problem with polite society—
As long as you don't perform the mudra of chicken,
As long as you don't proclaim like a duck,
As long as you don't float like a baby baboon.
Let us proclaim the lion's roar,
Let us fly like a seagull,
Let us shriek like an eagle:
Which reassures us that there is no maggot in our brains.
Let us proclaim in the name of delight and love and fearlessness.
We could eat our eggs and bacon happily ever after.

17 April 1978

78

SADDHARMA PUNSTERS

In the primordial world there is no language;
There is no need for translation.
In the manifested world there is the language of onomatopoeia.
In the fully evolved world we have languages of direct expression.
So we stumble, in this way:
The translator says, "What do you mean by ocean?"
The interpreter says, "I mean ocean."
The translator says, "What do you mean by ocean?"
The interpreter says, "I mean ocean,
Such as Mediterranean, Pacific, Atlantic, Indian, Antarctic—
On the whole I mean oceanic."
Then the translator says, "What do you mean by oceanic?"
The interpreter says, "I mean ocean-like."
And the translator says, "What do you mean by ocean-like?"
The interpreter says, "I mean salty, waves, divides continents, ships
    can sail through."
Then Robin Kornman says, "What do you mean by: Ships can sail
    through?"
The interpreter says, "Ships are miniature islands where people can
    stay, and they commute from one continent to another continent
    so that dry goods can be delivered."
Then Larry Mermelstein says, "What do you mean by dry goods?"
The interpreter says, "Dry goods means that they are dry because
    they are carried from mainland to mainland in ships without being
    spoiled by the water."
Lodrö Dorje says, "Ah, that makes sense!"
David Rome says, "There is a grammatical error in this language.
    Why do we have to say: Mainland to mainland? Since they have to
    travel by water, they are bound to get wet somewhat. Therefore
    we might say: From off the mainland on to the mainland. On the

whole, if the water is wet, why do we bother to say wet as
opposed to water? But on the other hand if water means wet,
why do we say water instead of saying wet? Why don't we use
one language? Either we should decide to say wet or water."
So the translators go on and the interpreters expound their thing
And one of these days, who's kidding who—
Whether skull means head or head means skull;
And we have confusion about why jackal is coyote or coyote is
    jackal;
And we have further problems: why worm is snake, and so forth.
Until the philosophy is carried out between translators and interpreters,
We will have to talk about why blue is not black,
Why a round earth,
Why the solar system.
So we end up agreeing with each other,
And the final agreement and conclusion between translators and
    interpreters is that the truth of suffering and the truth of prajna
    have no synonyms.
Let us be that way;
Let us understand those two,
So we can translate happily with the interpreter,
So we can interpret happily with the translator.
Iris is blue.
Blood is red.
Bone is white.
Marrow is grey.
When we look at the first sun we squint our eyes.
When we touch our finger to fire we go Ouch.
When we pee in the toilet, we assume a serious face.
When we wipe our bottoms, we assume a pragmatic look.
Let us translate that way;
Let us continue that way,
With or without Kornman Mermelstein Dorje Rome,
Happily ever after or sadly.
Let us translate fully.

The truth is:
When you say mind,
The translation is mind,
The interpretation is mind.
Good luck!

30 April 1978

79

I MISS YOU SO MUCH

I miss the Regent
And that transforms into clarity,
The luminosity which perpetually lights itself:
No need for switch or kindling wood.
I miss my son
And that transforms into energy,
Unyielding energy and play
Which can perform the cosmic dance.
I miss my queen
And that transforms into the power of speech,
Utterance of genuineness and nowness
Which cuts thoughts and proclaims the vision of indestructibility.
I miss the princess consort
And that transforms into passion;
Every moment becomes coemergent twist—
It is beyond coming or going.
The pain of the delight
Lights up the universe.
Choicelessly I remain as flaming vajra.

3 July 1978

Tro (*Happiness*)

148

80

THE DOHA OF CONFIDENCE
SAD SONG OF THE FOUR REMEMBRANCES

As I look constantly to the Great Eastern Sun,
Remembering the only father guru,
Overwhelming devotion blazes like a bonfire—
I, Chökyi Gyatso, remain alone.

Having been abandoned by my heart friends,
Though my feverish mind feels great longing,
It is joyful that I am sustained by this great confidence
Of the only father guru and the Great Eastern Sun.

Having seen the beauty of a mist covering the mountain,
The pines moving gently in the wind,
The firm power of rock-hard earth,
I am constantly reminded of the splendor and beauty
Of the only father guru and the Great Eastern Sun.

Wild flowers extend everywhere
On mountain meadows filled with the sweet smell of fragrant herbs.
Seeing the gentle deer frolicking from place to place,
I constantly remember the compassion and gentleness
Of the only father guru and the Great Eastern Sun.

Fighting enemies in the chasm of love and hate,
Having sharpened the weapon's point of joy and sorrow, hope and
      fear,
Seeing again and again these cowardly hordes,
I take refuge in the sole confidence
Of the only father guru and the Great Eastern Sun.

149

Fatherless, always dwelling in foreign lands,
Motherless, not hearing the speech of my own country,
Friendless, tears not quenching my thirst,
Remembering the warriors of the father and mother lineages,
I live alone in the sole blessing
Of the only father guru and the Great Eastern Sun.

25 July 1978

81

Bon Voyage

Bon Voyage.
You go away.
You go away with doves and rhododendrons.
You fade away in the memory that is part of the blue sky.
You will be forgotten with ashes of burning cigarettes,
As if fossils never formed in the prehistoric age.
Happy birthday to you.
You fade away in my life.

27 November 1978

82

MEMORIAL IN VERSE

This year of building the kingdom:
Dealing with the four seasons,
Studying how millet grows
And how the birds form their eggs;
Interested in studying how Tampax are made,
And how furniture can be gold-leafed;
Studying the construction of my home,
How the whitewash of the plain wood can be dignified,
How we could develop terry cloth on our floor,
How my dapöns can shoot accurately,
How my financiers can rush themselves into neurosis,
How the Board session can arrive at pragmatic decisions.
Oh, I have watched the sky grow old and the trees become younger
    as the seasons changed.
I have experienced the crisp air of December and January becoming a
    landmark of my life
As twenty grey hairs grow on my head.
I have witnessed that I have grown older and old,
As I grasp the scepters and handle the rice heaps, performing
    ceremonies.
I have thought I have also grown younger every day,
Taking showers, looking at myself in the mirror—
Perky and willing, I see myself:
That my lips don't quiver and my jaws are strong,
And my gaze is accurate.
When I think of this year, the most memorable occasion is the
    explosion of love affair,
Which was no joke;
It is true, I think of that every day

When I take my medicine for my good health, as prescribed by the
    physicians.
I think of my love affair as I wipe my bottom
Sitting on the toilet:
One appreciates that yellow dye sitting on white paper
As it flushes down the efficient American plumbing system.
One of this year's highlights is also that I failed and accomplished a
    lot:
The failure is mine,
The accomplishment is to my Regent.
Sometimes I think of the Ganges and Brahmaputra, or the Yellow
    River;
I could shed many tears.
And I think of the glaciers of Mt. Everest;
I could become solid, steady and stern—
I have developed the face of a frozen glacier.
So my life comes and goes in the same way the swallows sway back
    and forth in the air:
They may catch flies or they may not.
I have developed jurisdiction and fair constitution,
I have told the truth of the Great Eastern Sun vision from my moldy
    lips,
I have experienced certainty within uncertainty
Because one realizes the traffic of ants does not have traffic lights
And it is hard to give them speeding tickets.
My journey grows and shrinks.
However, the wicked will tremble and the awakened will rejoice.
I have fought, ambushed, raped, attacked, nursed, abused, cultivated,
    fed, nourished, hospitalized my world
With its world-ees.
Now I have grown very young and very old.
I appreciate the sun and moon, snow and rain, clouds, and deep blue
    sky;
I appreciate the ruggedness and the beauty of the universe,

Which is sometimes cruel, developing sharp thorns of the cactus
   plant,
And sometimes beautiful chrysanthemums of fantastic scent.
Blood or ink: both I take as yellow and purple color.

1 January 1979
Boulder, Colorado

83

TO MY SON

Be fearless and consume the ocean.
Take a sword and slay neurosis.
Climb the mountains of dignity and subjugate arrogance.
Look up and down and be decent.
When you learn to cry and laugh at the same time, with a gentle
     heart,
All my belongings are yours,
Including your father.
Happy birthday.

19 January 1979

FOR ANNE WALDMAN

When your blood boils,
Relax with the wind;
The wind always blows.
Play with a blade of grass;
The truth will always be told.

7 March 1979

PUTTING UP WITH THE TRANS-CANADA

The yearning Lake of Louise is imprisoned by her own ice;
The proud ranges of the Rockies are undermined by the bad weather;
An occasional avalanche protests from the glaciers.
But I am impressed that there is no outrage or complaint.
The trees and moss become very polite
And you can hear them talking to each other in hush hush, saying,
"Don't interrupt the mountains or the lake."
However, holiday-makers of the winter and the spring couldn't care
    less
About such diplomacy taking place between the mountains and the
    trees.
Japanese come a long way from Japan
And the locals intrude their weekends,
Taking advantage of the highway belt that cuts through the mountains,
Roaring with their motorized vehicles.
But the Canadian Rockies and the Canadian lakes are so naïve and
    stupid.
Supposing they heard the boom of prajna—
The Rockies might dissolve into sand dunes.
Let us not take a chance.
But, on the other hand, it is very tempting.

24 May 1979
Lake Louise, Alberta, Canada

BUDDHISM IN THE CANADIAN ROCKIES

With the walk of an elephant, the peacock's dance occurred;
With the gait of a jackal, the snake coils;
With the bark of a dog, a fleabite occurred.
Seeing the flower in the sky,
Experiencing blue sky,
We are never intimidated by the world of yes and no.
Tangerines are said to be good to eat,
Kumquats are cute;
However, we drink nectar without salt or sugar.
Go away, children of mud, disperse.
Don't look upon me as your playmate;
I have no desire to have a mud bath.
Roaring lion on the mountains
Parrots talking double language
Rhododendrons blooming too early because the season is unreliable—
The range of Himalayan mountains can dissolve with the Vajrayana
    magic;
All the oceans in the universe can dry up hearing the fantastic
    Vajrayana proclamation.
Children, children, don't be afraid;
Come along and join us:
As has been said, "Gathering nuts in May."
We will celebrate and cherish our heritage.
Infants that do not need bottles or nappies,
We go along to the archery range
To see the whistling arrows that sometimes hit and sometimes miss
    the target.
The impossibility of the possible can be achieved
At the archery ground of the playground.
Thick and grey clouds of rain and storm,

Desolate mountains which roar with avalanches—
Solitary hotel stands in the midst of nowhere,
Swarmed with holiday-makers with their multicolored outfits and
    seeming limps,
Armed with cameras, uniformed with sunshades,
Complaining, "Where is the Lake Louise?"—
Much to their own surprise,
Since they couldn't find delight anywhere, let alone in the Chateau
    or the Lake.
Canadian Rockies, extraordinary and blunt,
Decorated with snow caps and mist,
Proclaiming their dubious status range after range,
As if there were many weddings, but the couples never ate the cake;
As if there were many birthday celebrations, but the party is never
    finished.
Ironic sensationalism of the Canadian Rockies,
Young and blunt, treacherous but keen:
Shaggy reindeer descending along with mountain goats,
Feasting themselves on the garbage of the towns of Field or Banff—
As long as they are protected by the so-called national parksmanship,
    they are not hunted,
But at the same time they display subhuman immigrant greasy hair
    and tarred hooves.
Sun and moon shone simultaneously in the Canadian Rockies,
But I never saw them cheering up;
In fact, they usually cry along with the mist and clouds,
Wiping their tears with the local dust.
Somebody planted toothpick trees:
They grew and got older, decorated with little thorns and cones,
Inviting the holiday-makers,
Putting up with broken bottles and empty cans,
As if they were Boy Scouts who had lost their breakfast, lunch and
    dinner.
How splendid the Canadian Rockies—godless, without worshippers.

One wonders how we found ourselves in these Canadian Rockies,
Practicing meditation according to the example of Milarepa and our
    lineage.
We were able to get into the cracks in the skeleton of the CP
    administration;
They invited us because they had neither teeth nor veins to spare for
    themselves,
Thinking we might provide guts and fat and flesh for them.
How amazing that we could accommodate the Vajrayana world in
    the midst of this agitated poverty and business world.
Usually the merchants have no teeth, but they have very sharp
    gums;
They have no nails, but a tight grip.
Aren't we too brave? Sometimes I wonder.
Aren't we too cowardly? Sometimes I wonder.
Between the warrior and the coward, we find our path,
As lilies and frogs who never quarreled.
I take pride in the six smiles of the tiger
In this cuckooless world of North American atmosphere.
Spring never comes here, but autumn might be good;
In spite of the summer, we still take pleasure in the overwhelming
    winter:
It is a good time to practice.

24 May 1979

PRAISE TO THE LADY OF THE BIG HEART

For Lila Rich

Immeasurable space with primordial smile
Manifesting delight and beauty:
I appreciate your painful pleasure,
Our mutual humor, mutual passion, mutual goodness,
Together we ride the windhorse
With your elegant laughter echoing in all directions,
Even in the midst of a nightmare.
Your companionship, your genuine look, cause us to share our
    burdens together.
The great lady of the court, tireless, limitless—
I love your big heart.
I will be with you in life or death,
Along with your husband.
Cheerful birthday!

21 August 1979

NOT DECEIVING THE EARTH (and M. S. N.)

In protecting the earth, we found good pine needles and harsh dried
   wood along with rocks helpful.
When you begin to examine our earth,
You find tiny mushrooms and small grass blades,
Ornamented by the chatter of ground squirrels.
You find our soil is soft and rocky;
It does not permit artificial soil topping.
Our pine trees are diligent, dedicated and graceful;
In either life or death they will always perform their duty of
   pinetreeness,
Equipped with sap and bark.
We find our world of wilderness so refreshing.
Along with summer's drum, we produce occasional thundershowers,
   wet and dry messages:
We can't miss the point,
Since this earth is so bending and open to us, along with the rocks,
We are not shy,
We are so proud—
We can make a wound in a pine tree and it bleeds sap, and courts us,
   in spite of the setting-sun shadow;
They bend and serve so graciously, whether dead or alive.
We love our pines and rocks;
They are not covered with the superstitious setting-sun chemical
   manure of this and that.
We are so proud of the sky that we produce on our horizon.
Our stars twinkle and wink as if they know us;
We have no problem of recognition.
Our rocks and pine trees speak for us.
I love this soil—dusty, sandy, good, and free from astroturf:
Good earth, good grass, good pine tree, good Newton—

So good.
We love them all.
With them, we could bring about the Great Eastern Sun vision.

27 August 1979
Rocky Mountain Dharma Center

Drunken elephant

Drunken elephant—
Catching mirage by net;
In the mirror of my mind I comb my hair
With the brush of samsaric absurdity.

1979

LIMP AND TALK
For Ronald Stubbert

With the vision of the Great Eastern Sun
I limp and walk slowly,
Watching my P's and Q's,
Working for the liberation of beings.
Once I was taking a walk;
I stumbled over something
And I discovered you—
We became good friends.
Thank you for your loyalty and understanding:
I wish you a hearty happy birthday.

1979

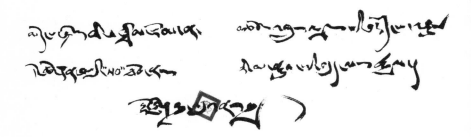

If you know "Not" and have discipline,
Then the ultimate "No" is attained,

Patience will arise along with exertion.
And you are victorious over the maras
of the setting sun.

HOW TO KNOW NO

There was a giant No.
That No rained.
That No created a tremendous blizzard.
That No made a dent on the coffee table.
That No was the greatest No of No's in the universe.
That No showered and hailed.
That No created sunshine, and simultaneous eclipse of the sun and
    moon.
That No was a lady's legs with nicely heeled shoes.
That No is the best No of all.
When a gentleman smiles, a good man,
That No is the beauty of his hips.
When you watch the gait of youths as they walk with alternating
    cheek rhythm,
When you watch their behinds,
That No is fantastic thighs, not fat or thin but taut in their strength,
Loveable or leaveable.
That No is shoulders that turn in or expand the chest, sad or happy,
Without giving in to a deep sigh.
That No is No of all No's.
Relaxation or restraint is in question.
Nobody knows that big No,
But we alone know that No.
This No is in the big sky, painted with sumi ink eternally.
This big No is tattooed on our genitals.
This big No is not purely freckles or birthmark,
But this big No is real big No.
Sky is blue,
Roses are red,
Violets are blue,

And therefore this big No is No.
Let us celebrate having that monumental No.
The monolithic No stands up and pierces heaven;
Therefore, monolithic No also spreads vast as the ocean.
Let us have great sunshine with this No No.
Let us have full moon with this No No.
Let us have cosmic No.
The cockroaches carry little No No's,
As well as giant elephants in African jungles—
Copulating No No and waltzing No No,
Guinea pig No No.
We find all the information and instructions when a mosquito buzzes.
We find some kind of No No.
Let our No No be the greatest motto:
No No for the king;
No No for the prime minister;
No No for the worms of our subjects.
Let us celebrate that our constipated dogs can relieve themselves
    freely in the name of No No.
Let us have No No so that Presbyterian preachers can have speech
    impediments in proclaiming No No.
Let our horses neigh No No.
Let the vajra sangha fart No No—
Giant No No that made a great imprint on the coffee table.

1 January 1980
The Kalapa Court
Boulder, Colorado

INTERNATIONAL AFFAIRS OF 1979
UNEVENTFUL BUT ENERGY-CONSUMING

Maybe Julius Caesar was right,
Organizing straight Roman roads throughout Europe.
Had the nose of Cleopatra been a different shape,
History might have changed.

This year is quite uneventful,
Regurgitating over and over that the nations have no chance to chew
    and eat a good meal.
The success of Joe Clark is replacement,
Adopting dog instead of cat as house pet in the Canadian Parliament.
Farewell to Pierre Trudeau;
His invitation to visit Tibet was comparable to the second visit of
    Nixon to China.
The pontiff's messages and declarations of good will are like having a
    pancake:
We know syrup will come along.
It is time for the Christians to unite:
Maybe the clean-shaven Catholics could join with the bearded Eas-
    tern church.
Margaret Thatcher's prime-ministership was frightening,
But turns out to be not so feisty.
We are reassured that she decided to wear a skirt as opposed to
    trousers—
What a relief.
Tories always tame ladies,
And the Liberals and Labor party wish they had a she-leader who
    could wear riding breeches.
However, England will be always England:
When she is sad, she becomes tough;

When she is tough, she becomes soft.
Good old glory is fading,
And now they refer to the kingdom as ruled by Britannia, as opposed to Elizabeth the Second.
We are sad at the death of Uncle Dicky;
He was such a good person, but he had to pay his karmic debt:
Instead of being killed on board the ship *Kelly*,
He was destroyed on a fishing boat—
May he be reborn as a Shambhalian warrior.
Vietnam invasion of Cambodia,
China invasion of Vietnam:
All of those jokes are comparable to a group of lizards biting each others' tails.
Where is the spirit of communism?
Marx, Engels, Lenin—
If they returned and saw what a mess they made in the universe, they would be horrified.
We find nobody is practicing true communism.
The Chinese declaration of religious freedom in Tibet is humorous:
You are free not to practice religion,
And the Panchen Lama beckons the Dalai Lama.
Opening the door of Sino-Tibetan tourism fooled the sharpest and most professional journalists;
They lost their critical intelligence.
Islamic tradition is fantastic:
"Killing enemy, develop wealth in the name of Allah."
The grand Ayatollah declares spiritual principles in the name of hate,
Recapturing the example of *Jaws*.
Sino-American declaration is sweet and sour,
Missing the Hunan beef of Mao Tse Tung,
Both parties not knowing how to handle their power;
Taiwan takes secret delight that it does not have to maintain international law and order.
Korea lost its leader,
Park killed in a parking lot by his own security guards;

Unifying South and North Chao Xian to make Korea out of Korea
    is questionable.

In short, the nations are capitalizing on what they were;
In turn they lose what they are.
This year is not an exciting year at all,
In spite of short dramas and quick exchanges.
There could be an exciting perspective to it:
Declaration of war between Islam and the rest of the faiths.
The Shah as *le chat* got out of the bag,
Terrified, frustrated—we feel sorry for the Empress Farah.
We realize that the United Nations is a rib cage without heartbeat or
    lungs,
Trying to do its best.
In spite of China being chairman of the Security Council,
Nothing gets done.
We are sad;
It is hopeless.
We are happy;
We could contribute.
The state of affairs of the world is somewhat better than a male dog
    pissing on an appropriate bush.

1 January 1980

TO THE NOBLE SANGHA

With your doubt, laziness, hesitation and inquisitiveness,
We have found magnificent soil in which to sow the seed of the
buddhadharma.
With your friendliness, sense of humor and willingness to work with
me,
We are able to harvest our crop.
Your sympathy and genuineness led me to believe that true dharma
can be established in North America.
The ten years of my existence here have been long and treacherous;
Yet it is short—as if it happened yesterday.
I appreciate you all:
Without your exertion and delight I would have passed away long
ago.
That is your best birthday present:
That you will practice with me.

9 February 1980
Denver, Colorado

A countertoast at a celebration of the author's birthday.

FISHING WISELY

From the samsaric ocean,
With the net of your good posture,
The fish of your subconscious gossip
Are exposed to the fresh air.
No praise, no blame.
The fish of your subconscious mind
Look for samsaric air,
But they die in coemergent wisdom.

25 February 1980

95

MISCELLANEOUS DOHA

Unborn rock
Petrified sky
Crippled windhorse
Mute skull
Blue red—
If you cannot sort them out,
Don't cut your tongue on the razor smeared with honey:
Rejoice in dancing on a needle.

28 April 1980

EXPOSÉ
ACKNOWLEDGING ACCUSATIONS IN THE NAME OF DEVOTION

Remember, O Tusum Khyenpa!
Remember, O Father Karma Pakshi!
Remember, O Tilopa!
Remember, O Naropa!
Remember, O Milarepa!
Remember, O Marpa Lotsawa!
When I remember your kindness and your power,
I am left in the midst of the dark-age dungeon.
When I taste your great bliss,
It is as if for the first time—
As if no one had tasted honey before.
When I realize your devotion,
It makes me so lonely.
When I see and experience anything good and wonderful,
It reminds me of the Kagyü wisdom and what you have sacrificed
    for us.
When I put on good clothing or see an attractive maiden,
When I handle gold or diamond,
I feel great pain and love for your wisdom and exertion.
I can only cry,
Your beauty and exertion and footprints make me so sad and full of
    longing—
Because we are left behind, nowhere,
Unable even to see your footprints in the dust.
How could you do such a thing?
Any mark of elegance or imprint of goodness;
For that matter, anything wicked and raw, confused or destructive;
Anything we see makes us feel so sad.
We will cry after the Father Kagyü,

Whether we are attacked or praised,
We do not follow the conventional pattern of hope and fear;
Nonetheless, you left us alone.
We feel so sad and lonely,
We want to taste you, smell you—
Where are you?
We cry and we would like to threaten you and say:
Show us your true face, to help us never give up;
In this very bed, on this very cushion, in this very room—
If you don't show us your face and tell us,
We will perish in tears and dissolve in misery.
Please come and be with us.
At least look at us the way we are,
Which may not be the best you expect of us;
But we have the greatest devotion,
Beyond your preconceptions.
We will cry and shed our tears until our eyeballs drop in the sand
    dune
And we drown in the ocean of our tears.
O Knower of the Three Times, omniscient,
We have tried and practiced after your example:
Please don't give up.
When we iron our clothes, it is for you.
When we shine our shoes, it is for you.
When we wear jewelry, it is for you.
We do everything because of you;
We have no personal concern.
If we do not realize your dignity and wisdom,
May we rot and dissolve into dust.
We do everything for your sake and because of you.
We are so sad because of you,
We are so joyful because of you.
Father, if you have strength, this is the time to manifest.
I am about to die
And be reborn in crying and laughing at the same time.

Father, please have consideration for us.
We do not do anything for our own sake.
We do everything for the sake of devotion to you.

30 April 1980

97

MIXED GRILL DHARMA SERVED WITH BURGUNDY OF GROUND MAHAMUDRA 1980 VINTAGE

THE ELEGANT FEAST OF TIMELESS ACCURACY

Blond cactus thorn with occasional freckles,
Albino chimpanzees with oy vey mantra,
Rock or diamond,
Shoes or socks,
Food or excrement—
These dichotomies dissolve and pop up.
As you teach Vajrayana to the Americans,
Sometimes they reduce into tadpoles;
Other times they expand into crocodiles that you find in South
    America.
Inconceivable mind finds a way around, and very direct, to hug
    them and puncture them.
Pollution is not a question.
Build a magnificent granite castle;
Build a magnificent Aberdeen granite castle on the tip of your own
    tongue.
Buy the Windsor castle, brick by brick,
As the ticks of your watch move, second by second,
Black-blue dial on your wrist.
Shave the mustache of King George
By explaining to him the scientific discoveries of poison oak.
Round needle of Rahula can create eclipse of sun and moon
    simultaneously.
Provide prana dot by putting together mixing and melting.
Bind the world with a single strand of horsehair from Maestoso
    Drala.

Make the universe murky white
And feed the six realms with honey and milk through the straws of
    porcupines' quills.
Act unreasonable,
As if tigers from Bengal are in debt at the House of Pancakes.
The Catholics' cherubs supposedly transcend their nappies;
However, they are eating too many grapes provided by the Italian
    Communist party chief to the Vatican City.
Some day we hope the haggis will walk.
One day the potatoes will play their harps in the name of the glories
    of Ireland.
Too much has been said here.
I hope this achieves the result of too little being said here.
After all, splinter is not harpoon;
Elegant burp is not resounding fart.
I hope this world will live up to what it proclaims;
Otherwise, we have a shattering surprise:
Sooner or later we end up picking up the small pieces.
With tremendous yearning towards sea urchins' eggs,
I congratulate this world made out of this and that, that and this.
It is very impressive that everyone knows the morning sun will set in
    the evening and there will be another sun shining the next day.
I find people are so smart—they can talk about tomorrow and plan
    ahead.
How clever they are—assuming they know there is a next day.
Such brilliant and noble naïveté is good.
It seems that people know, if there is light, there will be dark:
I am utterly amazed at their insight.
Glory be to the mosquitoes;
Glory be to the thorny rose.
Fire can burn;
Water can quench thirst.
Amazingly, it seems that this universe works.
So fortunate.

Past present future in us may teach us the true dharma,
Without a sneeze or too many hiccups.
May the wheel of dharma revolve eternally in the name of the Great
Eastern Sun.

4 May 1980

98

GROWING PAINS ARE OVER
For David Rome

Once you were a wounded warrior:
Now you have developed fearlessness, you can play with the sword
    blade.
Once you were a coward and wouldn't talk to strangers;
Now you have learned to declare the command of the Great Eastern
    Sun.
Once you were miserly:
Now you can spend great energy, free from taking breaks.
We appreciate you—
Please accept this bow, representing upaya;
Please take this arrow, representing prajna.
We wish that you may continuously protect the command
And generate the wisdom of the Rigden Fathers.
Cheerful birthday!

17 June 1980

99

COMING OF AGE OF MY SON
For the Vajra Regent Ösel Tendzin

You have been placed in the cradle of loving kindness,
And suckled with the profound and brilliant milk of eternal
  doubtlessness.
In the cool shade of fearlessness,
You have been fanned with the fan of joy and happiness.
As you grew older,
With various displays of phenomena,
We led you to the self-existing playground.
As you grew up,
To promote the primordial confidence,
We led you to the archery range of the warriors.
As you developed further,
We showed you human society, which possesses beauty and dignity.
You, a true warrior, matured,
Developing eternally youthful confidence without beginning or end.
We take pride in you, that you have witnessed the Great Eastern
  Sun.

Sometimes we worry about you:
How we can ward off the evils of the setting sun.
Other times we appreciate you:
You are a true manifestation of our vision.
We request you to become more merciful,
And we rejoice that you are the dharma heir.
Let us join heaven and earth together.
O, Ösel Tendzin,
Our profound love and gratitude is expressed on this occasion.
In the name of the lineage,
In the name of the Vajradhatu sangha,

In the name of myself and my wife—
Thank you for being as you are.
Please be good.
Cheerful birthday!

10 July 1980

Da (*Moon*)

184

100

YOU MIGHT BE TIRED OF THE SEAT THAT YOU DESERVE

For the Vajra Regent at Midsummer's Day

Dearly loved comrade,
If you do not hold the seat,
Others may take it away;
If you do not sit on a rock,
It becomes mushy clay;
If you don't have patience to sit on a rock or seat,
They give you away;
If you are not diligent in holding the throne,
Some opportunist will snatch it away;
If you are tired of your seat,
Some interior decorator will rearrange it;
If you don't have a throne,
You cannot speak or proclaim from it,
So the audience will dissipate;
If you don't have a government seat to sit on,
Your wisdom and command seal will be snatched by others;
If you run around, thinking that you have a seat to come back to,
It will be washed away by the turbulent river,
Like a presidential platform;
You can never proclaim your command:
Either it will be disassembled by the cockroaches
Or the frivolous multitude will take it away as souvenirs.

It may be hard to sit on the seat,
But one must endure it.
Do sit on your seat,
Whether it is hard or soft.
Once you sit on your seat,

The sitting itself becomes truly command and message;
Then, undoubtedly, multitudes of people will respect and obey it
As the vajra throne of Bodhgaya where Buddha taught.
Truth becomes exertion.
The message of hard fact proclaims itself,
So you don't have to emphasize harder truth.
Offering your seat in order to please others will not give authentic
    reward—
They will take the attitude that you are a pleasant seat-offerer.
So, my son, please don't move around;
Assume your seat, and sit, and be.
If you be that way, truth prevails;
Command is heard throughout the land.
So sit and hold your seat.
Then you will enjoy, because others will admire you.
This is hard to do, but easy to accomplish.

21 June 1981

101

When I ride a horse

When I ride a horse,
I hold my seat.
When I play with snakes,
I snap them on my wrist.
When I play with dangerous maidens,
I let them talk first.

2 July 1981

102

TIMELY INNUENDO
For Loppön Lodrö Dorje

The burning heart of reality kindles the twigs of awesome truth.
Men's fate depends on their actions.
Mysticism is plumage on one's hat.
Let us dance with the Loppön!
Your devotion and wisdom are certainly worthy of praise.

18 August 1981

A HEART LOST AND DISCOVERED

If there is no full moon in the sky,
How is it possible to see the reflection in the pond?
If the tiger has sharp claws,
How is it possible not to use them?
How could we bake our bread
If there were no fire?
At the death of the Karmapa we become softened and devotional.
It is true,
Those who have never cried in their lives, cry this time,
And shed tears that will water the earth:
So, we can produce further flowers and greenery.

14 November 1981

On the death of His Holiness Rangjung Rikpe Dorje, the Sixteenth Gyalwa Karmapa.

104

COMMAND

Nuclear catastrophe is imminent;
Man's aggression to kill himself or others is imminent;
Tiger hates his or her stripes and is going to untiger;
Yet Karmapa never left a declaration of independence.
The Kagyü kingdom is intact,
If not totally packaged by Vajradhatu of North America.
I am so sad, so devastated,
I feel I have lost my head;
But I have gained a new head, a Karmapa head.
For better or worse I will rule according to Karmapa's imperial
    command:
I will remain as the Emperor of Kalapa.
We still allow people to smile and grin:
Human beings' habitual patterns are obviously the best of their
    ability to create a society of their own,
Whether they are tiger, lion, yak or buffalo.
We like America in its buffaloness:
Let America be buffalo kingdom, in spite of the unicorns.
Cheerio, as we say in Britain.
You deserve your cheerfulness, nonetheless.

20 December 1981
Boulder, Colorado

Composed during a ceremony marking the cremation of the Sixteenth Karmapa.

GOLDEN SUN
For Shibata Kanjuro XX, Archery Master

In this land of *kami-no-yama,* I still miss you.
We are all longing for your wisdom.
As you know, we have lost our leader the Karmapa,
But it is comforting to have you as good friend and teacher.
The mirror has never stopped reflecting,
The *kiku* has never stopped blossoming;
Yumi still twangs
Ya still fly:
Our students constantly practice and look forward to your further
    teaching.
I, your friend, am getting old and sick,
But still my heart's blood turns into liquid iron.
The strength of appreciation for the warrior heritage
Is part of my metallic blood,
And my bones are made out of meteoric iron.

Profound respect to you, Sensei, on your birthday:
May the Great Eastern Sun continuously arise in your life, with
    happiness and prosperity.

29 December 1981

106

As skylarks hunt for their prey

As skylarks hunt for their prey,
I am captured by their stillness.

I experience neither thirst nor hunger,
But skylarks captivate my memory.

Whistling arrows on the battlefield remind me of my general's bravery:
Should I run away or should I stay?

Buddhism neither tells me the false nor the true:
It allows me to discover myself.

Shakyamuni was so silent:
Should I complain against him?

31 December 1981

SEASONS' GREETINGS

Emerging to the surface,
Such virginity
Blossoming as a teenager—
Wish I was Spring's father.

As the thunder gathers rain,
Flowers drink water;
Arrogant greenery has no hesitation.
Summer provides festivity, and life is worth living.

Hot pregnant mother
Preparing the eggs and sperm for the next year:
So voluptuous and ostentatious.
O Autumn, I will never go to bed with you,
But you come to dinner with me.

Constriction and rigidity of your martial law do not frighten me,
You give me chills and shivers;
But the way you decorate the mountains—
I admire your extravaganza.

9 May 1983

THE MEEK
POWERFULLY NONCHALANT AND DANGEROUSLY
SELF-SATISFYING

In the midst of thick jungle
Monkeys swing,
Snakes coil,
Days and nights go by.
Suddenly I witness you,
Striped like sun and shade put together.
You slowly scan and sniff, perking your ears,
Listening to the creeping and rustling sounds:
You have supersensitive antennae.
Walking gently, roaming thoroughly,
Pressing paws with claws,
Moving with the sun's camouflage,
Your well-groomed exquisite coat has never been touched or ham-
    pered by others.
Each hair bristles with a life of its own.
In spite of your feline bounciness and creeping slippery accomplish-
    ment,
Pretending to be meek,
You drool as you lick your mouth.
You are hungry for prey—
You pounce like a young couple having orgasm;
You teach zebras why they are black and white;
You surprise haughty deer, instructing them to have a sense of humor
    along with their fear.
When you are satisfied roaming in the jungle,
You pounce as the agent of the sun:
Catching pouncing clawing biting sniffing—
Such meek tiger achieves his purpose.

Glory be to the meek tiger
Roaming, roaming endlessly.
Pounce, pounce in the artful meek way,
Licking whiskers with satisfying burp.
Oh, how good to be tiger!

13 May 1983

The text of this book was set in Mergenthaler Linotron by Jackson Typesetting Co., Inc., Jackson, Michigan. It was printed and bound by McNaughton & Gunn Lithographers, Saline, Michigan. The limited cloth edition was bound by Kingsport Press, Kingsport, Tennessee. Design by Hazel Bercholz